The Low-Sodium Slow Cooker Cookbook:
250 Heart Healthy Recipes for Balanced Low-Salt Meals

Diana Parker

Disclaimer:

All information and resources found in this book are based on the opinions of
the author. All information is intended to motivate readers to make their own
health, nutrition, and fitness decisions after consulting with their health care
provider. The macro plans are not medically-prescribed diets. The focus is meal
prep education and recipe ideas.

We encourage you to consult a doctor before making any health or diet changes,
especially any changes related to a specific diagnosis or condition. NO
information in this book should be used to diagnose, treat, prevent, or cure any
disease or condition

Table of Contents

Breakfast

Zucchini Oatmeal

Preparation time: 10 minutes
Cooking time: 8 hours
Servings: 4

Ingredients:
- ½ cup oatmeal
- 1 carrot, grated
- 1 ½ cups coconut milk
- ¼ zucchini, grated
- ½ teaspoon cinnamon
- 2 tablespoons honey
- ¼ cup pecans, chopped

Directions:
1. In your Slow cooker, mix oats with carrot, coconut milk, zucchini, cloves, nutmeg, cinnamon, and honey, stir, cover, and cook on Low for 8 hours.
2. Add pecans, toss, divide into bowls and serve.

per serving: 360 calories, 4.9g protein, 24.2g carbohydrates, 29.7g fat, 4.8g fiber, 0mg cholesterol, 26mg sodium, 405mg potassium.

Apple Rice

Preparation time: 10 minutes
Cooking time: 7 hours
Servings: 9

Ingredients:
- 4 apples, cored, peeled, and chopped
- 2 tablespoons coconut oil
- 2 teaspoons cinnamon
- 1 ½ cups brown rice
- ½ teaspoon vanilla extract
- ¼ teaspoon ground nutmeg
- 5 cups of coconut milk

Directions:
1. In the Slow cooker, put apples, cinnamon, rice, vanilla, nutmeg, and coconut milk, cover, cook on Low for 7 hours, stir, divide into bowls and serve for breakfast.

per serving: 501 calories, 5.7g protein, 45.7g carbohydrates, 35.9g fat, 6.7g fiber, 0mg cholesterol, 22mg sodium, 5mg potassium.

Banana Mix

Preparation time: 10 minutes
Cooking time: 6 hours
Servings: 8

Ingredients:
- 2 cups quinoa
- 2 bananas, mashed
- 4 cups of water
- 2 cups blueberries
- 2 teaspoons vanilla extract
- 2 tablespoons honey
- 1 teaspoon ground cinnamon
- Cooking spray

Directions:
1. Grease your Slow cooker with cooking spray, add quinoa, bananas, water, blueberries, vanilla, maple syrup, and cinnamon, stir, cover, and cook on Low for 6 hours.
2. Stir again, divide into bowls and serve for breakfast.

per serving: 223 calories,6.6g protein, 44g carbohydrates,2.8g fat, 4.8g fiber, 0mg cholesterol, 7mg sodium, 380mg potassium.

Vanilla Quinoa

Preparation time: 10 minutes
Cooking time: 4 hours
Servings: 4

Ingredients:
- 1 cup quinoa
- 2 cups of coconut milk
- 2 cups of water
- ¼ cup stevia
- 1 teaspoon ground cinnamon
- 1 teaspoon vanilla extract

Directions:
1. In your Slow cooker, mix quinoa with milk, water, stevia, cinnamon, and vanilla, stir, cover, cook on Low for 3 hours and 30 minutes, stir, cook for 30 minutes more, divide into bowls, and serve for breakfast.

per serving: 437 calories,8.8g protein, 34.5g carbohydrates, 31.2g fat, 5.9g fiber, 0mg cholesterol, 24mg sodium, 560mg potassium.

Quinoa with Fruits

Preparation time: 10 minutes
Cooking time: 10 hours
Servings: 6

Ingredients:
- ¾ cup quinoa
- ¾ cup oatmeal
- 2 tablespoons honey
- 1 cup apricots, chopped
- 6 cups of water
- 1 teaspoon vanilla extract
- ¾ cup hazelnuts, chopped

Directions:
1. In your Slow cooker, mix quinoa with oats honey, apricots, water, vanilla, and hazelnuts, stir, cover, and cook on Low for 10 hours.
2. Stir quinoa mix again divides into bowls, and serve for breakfast.

per serving: 212 calories,6.1g protein, 30.8g carbohydrates, 7.8g fat, 3.9g fiber, 0mg cholesterol, 10mg sodium, 294mg potassium.

Blueberry Oatmeal

Preparation time: 10 minutes
Cooking time: 8 hours
Servings: 4

Ingredients:
- ½ cup quinoa
- 1 cup oatmeals
- 1 teaspoon vanilla extract
- 5 cups of water
- Zest of 1 lemon, grated
- 1 teaspoon vanilla extract
- 2 tablespoons flaxseed
- 1 tablespoon coconut oil
- 3 tablespoons honey
- 1 cup blueberries

Directions:
1. In your Slow cooker, mix quinoa, water, oats, vanilla, lemon zest, flaxseed, honey, and blueberries, stir, cover, and cook on Low for 8 hours.
2. Divide into bowls and serve for breakfast.

per serving: 275 calories,6.7g protein, 46.8g carbohydrates, 7.3g fat, 5.4g fiber, 0mg cholesterol, 13mg sodium, 263mg potassium.

Chai Quinoa

Preparation time: 10 minutes
Cooking time: 6 hours
Servings: 6

Ingredients:

- 1 cup quinoa
- 1 egg white
- 2 cups of coconut milk
- ¼ teaspoon vanilla extract
- 1 tablespoon honey
- ¼ teaspoon cardamom, ground
- ¼ teaspoon ginger, grated
- ¼ teaspoon ground cinnamon
- ¼ teaspoon vanilla extract
- ¼ teaspoon nutmeg, ground
- 1 tablespoon coconut flakes

Directions:

1. In your Slow cooker, mix quinoa with egg white, milk, vanilla, honey, cardamom, ginger, cinnamon, vanilla, and nutmeg, stir a bit, cover and cook on Low for 6 hours. Stir, divide into bowls, and serve for breakfast with coconut flakes on top.

per serving: 307 calories, 6.5g protein, 25.9g carbohydrates, 21.1g fat, 5.2g fiber, 0mg cholesterol, 19mg sodium, 387mg potassium.

Quinoa Bake

Preparation time: 10 minutes
Cooking time: 7 hours
Servings: 5

Ingredients:

- 1 cup quinoa
- 4 tablespoons olive oil
- 2 cups of water
- ½ cup dates, chopped
- 3 bananas, chopped
- ¼ cup coconut, shredded
- 2 teaspoons ground cinnamon
- 2 tablespoons honey
- 1 cup walnuts, toasted and chopped

Directions:

1. Put the oil in your Slow cooker, add quinoa, water, dates, bananas, coconut, cinnamon, honey, and walnuts, stir, cover, and cook on Low for 7 hours.
2. Divide into bowls and serve for breakfast.

per serving: 531 calories, 12.2g protein, 62.1g carbohydrates, 29.7g fat, 8.2g fiber, 0mg cholesterol, 7mg sodium, 716mg potassium.

Butterscotch Pudding

Preparation time: 10 minutes
Cooking time: 1 hour and 40 minutes
Servings: 6

Ingredients:
- 2 oz coconut oil
- 2 ounces honey
- 7 ounces almond flour
- ½ cup of coconut milk
- 1 teaspoon vanilla extract
- Zest of ½ lemon, grated
- Cooking spray
- 1 egg

Directions:
1. In a bowl, mix honey, milk, vanilla, lemon zest, and eggs and whisk well.
2. Add flour and whisk well again.
3. Grease your Slow cooker with cooking spray, add pudding mix, spread, cover, and cook on High for 1 hour and 30 minutes.
4. Divide between plates and serve for breakfast.

per serving: 301 calories,6.1g protein, 13.8g carbohydrates, 25.4g fat, 2.8g fiber, 27mg cholesterol, 22mg sodium, 68mg potassium.

French Pudding

Preparation time: 10 minutes
Cooking time: 1 hour and 30 minutes
Servings: 4

Ingredients:
- 3 egg yolks
- 6 ounces coconut cream
- 1 teaspoon vanilla extract
- 2 tablespoons honey

Directions:
1. In a bowl, mix the egg yolks with honey and whisk well.
2. Add Greek-style yogurt and vanilla extract, whisk well, pour into your 4 ramekins, place them in your Slow cooker, add some water to the slow cooker, cover and cook on High for 1 hour and 30 minutes.
3. Leave aside to cool down and serve.

per serving: 173 calories,3g protein, 11.6g carbohydrates, 13.5g fat, 1g fiber, 157mg cholesterol, 13mg sodium, 133mg potassium.

Coconut Milk Breakfast

Preparation time: 5 minutes
Cooking time: 3 hours
Servings: 5

Ingredients:
- 1 teaspoon ground cinnamon
- ½ teaspoon nutmeg, ground
- ½ cup almonds, chopped
- 1 teaspoon honey
- 1.5 cup of coconut milk
- ¼ teaspoon cardamom, ground
- ¼ teaspoon cloves, ground

Directions:
1. In your Slow cooker, mix the coconut milk with cinnamon, nutmeg, almonds, honey, cardamom, and cloves, stir, cover, cook on Low for 3 hours, divide into bowls and serve for breakfast

per serving: 228 calories,3.7g protein, 7.8g carbohydrates, 22g fat, 3.1g fiber, 0mg cholesterol, 11mg sodium, 265mg potassium.

Carrot and Walnut Pudding

Preparation time: 10 minutes
Cooking time: 8 hours
Servings: 4

Ingredients:
- 4 carrots, grated
- 1 ½ cups coconut milk
- ½ teaspoon ground cinnamon
- 2 tablespoons honey
- ¼ cup walnuts, chopped
- 1 teaspoon vanilla extract

Directions:
1. In your Slow cooker, mix carrots with milk, cloves, nutmeg, cinnamon, honey, walnuts, and vanilla extract, stir, cover, and cook on Low for 8 hours.
2. Divide into bowls and serve for breakfast.

per serving: 313 calories,4.5g protein, 20.6g carbohydrates, 26.1g fat, 4.2g fiber, 0mg cholesterol, 56mg sodium, 479mg potassium.

Ginger Bowls

Preparation time: 10 minutes
Cooking time: 6 hours
Servings: 3

Ingredients:

- 2 apples, cored, peeled, and cut into medium chunks
- 1 tablespoon honey
- 1 tablespoon ginger, grated
- 1 cup of coconut milk
- ¼ teaspoon ground cinnamon
- ½ teaspoon vanilla extract
- ¼ teaspoon cardamom, ground

Directions:

1. In your slow cooker, combine the apples with the honey, ginger, and the other ingredients, toss, put the lid on, and cook on Low for 6 hours.
2. Divide into bowls and serve for breakfast.

per serving: 292 calories, 2.4g protein, 32.4g carbohydrates, 19.5g fat, 5.8g fiber, 0mg cholesterol, 14mg sodium, 401mg potassium.

Apple Butter

Preparation time: 10 minutes
Cooking time: 4 hours
Servings: 2

Ingredients:

- 2 apples, cored, peeled, and pureed
- ½ cup coconut cream
- 2 tablespoons apple cider
- 2 tablespoons honey
- ¼ teaspoon ground cinnamon
- ½ teaspoon lemon juice
- ¼ teaspoon ginger, grated

Directions:

1. In your slow cooker, mix the apple puree with the cream, honey, and the other ingredients, whisk, put the lid on and cook on High for 4 hours.
2. Blend using an immersion blender, cool down, and serve for breakfast.

per serving: 327 calories, 2.1g protein, 53.7g carbohydrates, 14.7g fat, 7g fiber, 0mg cholesterol, 13mg sodium, 432mg potassium.

Cherries Oats

Preparation time: 10 minutes
Cooking time: 7 hours
Servings: 2

Ingredients:
- 1 cup organic almond milk
- ½ cup oatmeal
- 1 tablespoon cocoa powder
- ½ cup cherries pitted
- 2 tablespoons honey
- ¼ teaspoon vanilla extract

Directions:
1. In your slow cooker, mix the organic almond milk with the cherries and the other ingredients, toss, put the lid on and cook on Low for 7 hours.
2. Divide into 2 bowls and serve for breakfast.

per serving: 438 calories, 6.2g protein, 42.8g carbohydrates, 30.3g fat, 6.1g fiber, 0mg cholesterol, 23mg sodium, 468mg potassium

Cashew and Lemon Zest Butter

Preparation time: 10 minutes
Cooking time: 4 hours
Servings: 4

Ingredients:
- 1 cup cashews, soaked overnight, drained and blended
- ½ cup coconut cream
- ¼ teaspoon ground cinnamon
- 1 teaspoon lemon zest, grated
- 2 tablespoons honey
- A pinch of ginger, ground

Directions:
1. In your slow cooker, mix the cashews with the cream and the other ingredients, whisk, put the lid on and cook on High for 4 hours.
2. Blend using an immersion blender, divide into jars, and serve for breakfast cold.

per serving: 298 calories, 6g protein, 21.7g carbohydrates, 23g fat, 1.8g fiber, 0mg cholesterol, 10mg sodium, 280mg potassium.

Maple Syrup Quinoa

Preparation time: 10 minutes
Cooking time: 8 hours
Servings: 2

Ingredients:
- ½ cup quinoa
- 2 cups of coconut milk
- 1 tablespoon maple syrup
- 1 teaspoon vanilla extract
- 2 tablespoons raisins
- ¼ cup blackberries

Directions:
1. In your slow cooker, mix the quinoa with the milk, maple syrup, and the other ingredients, toss, put the lid on and cook on Low for 8 hours.
2. Divide into 2 bowls and serve for breakfast.

per serving: 775 calories,12g protein, 56.5g carbohydrates, 60g fat, 9.6g fiber, 0mg cholesterol, 41mg sodium, 991mg potassium.

Peach and Oats Mix

Preparation time: 10 minutes
Cooking time: 8 hours
Servings: 2

Ingredients:
- ½ cup steel cut oats
- 2 cups organic almond milk
- ½ cup peaches pitted and roughly chopped
- ½ teaspoon vanilla extract
- 1 teaspoon cinnamon powder

Directions:
1. In your slow cooker, mix the oats with the almond milk, peaches, and the other ingredients, toss, put the lid on and cook on Low for 8 hours.
2. Divide into bowls and serve for breakfast right away.

per serving: 125 calories,3.5g protein, 21.5g carbohydrates, 2.7g fat, 3.2g fiber, 0mg cholesterol, 76mg sodium, 237mg potassium.

Almond Bowls

Preparation time: 10 minutes
Cooking time: 5 hours
Servings: 4

Ingredients:

- 1 cup quinoa
- 2 cups organic almond milk
- 2 tablespoons olive oil, melted
- 2 tablespoons of liquid honey
- A pinch of cinnamon powder
- A pinch of nutmeg, ground
- ¼ cup almonds, sliced
- Cooking spray

Directions:

1. Grease your slow cooker with the cooking spray, add the quinoa, milk, melted olive oil, and the other ingredients, toss, put the lid on and cook on Low for 5 hours.
2. Divide the mix into bowls and serve for breakfast.

per serving: 298 calories,7.5g protein, 39.2g carbohydrates, 13.2g fat, 4g fiber, 0mg cholesterol, 40mg sodium, 333mg potassium.

Fruits and Honey Oatmeal

Preparation time: 10 minutes
Cooking time: 10 hours
Servings: 4

Ingredients:

- 2 tablespoons olive oil
- 2 tablespoons of liquid honey
- 4 apples, cored, peeled, and chopped
- 2 cups old-fashioned oats
- 1 and ½ tablespoons cinnamon powder
- 4 cups of water

Directions:

1. Spread olive oil in your Slow cooker.
2. Add honey, apples, oats, cinnamon, and water, cover, and cook on Low for 8 hours.
3. Stir oatmeal, divide into bowls, and serve for breakfast.

per serving: 358 calories,5.9g protein, 66.5g carbohydrates, 10g fat, 9.4g fiber, 0mg cholesterol, 12mg sodium, 391mg potassium.

Quinoa Mix

Preparation time: 10 minutes
Cooking time: 7 hours
Servings: 6

Ingredients:
- ½ cup quinoa
- 1 and ½ cups steel cut oats
- 4 and ½ cups of organic almond milk
- 3 tablespoons honey
- 1 and ½ teaspoons vanilla extract
- Cooking spray

Directions:
1. Grease your Slow cooker with cooking spray, add quinoa, oats, almond milk, honey, and vanilla extract, cover, and cook on Low for 7 hours.
2. Stir, divide into bowls, and serve for breakfast.

per serving: 172 calories,4.9g protein, 32.9g carbohydrates, 2.6g fat, 3.3g fiber, 0mg cholesterol, 27mg sodium, 189mg potassium.

Pumpkin Oatmeal

Preparation time: 10 minutes
Cooking time: 9 hours
Servings: 4

Ingredients:
- Cooking spray
- 1 cup steel-cut oats
- ½ cup organic almond milk
- 4 cups of water
- 2 tablespoons honey
- ½ cup pumpkin puree
- ½ teaspoon cinnamon powder
- A pinch of cloves, ground
- A pinch of ginger, grated
- A pinch of allspice, ground
- A pinch of nutmeg, ground

Directions:
1. Grease your Slow cooker with cooking spray, add oats, milk, water, honey, pumpkin puree, cinnamon, cloves, ginger, allspice, and nutmeg, cover, and cook on Low for 9 hours.
2. Stir your oatmeal, divide into bowls and serve for breakfast.

per serving: 99 calories,2.1g protein, 20.1g carbohydrates, 1.6g fat, 2.2g fiber, 0mg cholesterol, 49mg sodium, 157mg potassium.

Quinoa Bars

Preparation time: 10 minutes
Cooking time: 4 hours
Servings: 8

Ingredients:

- 2 tablespoons of liquid honey
- 2 tablespoons olive oil
- Cooking spray
- ½ teaspoon cinnamon powder
- 1 cup organic almond milk
- 2 eggs
- ½ cup raisins
- 1/3 cup quinoa
- 1/3 cup almonds, toasted and chopped
- 1/3 cup dried apples, chopped
- 2 tablespoons chia seeds

Directions:

1. In a bowl, mix almond olive oil with maple syrup, cinnamon, milk, eggs, quinoa, raisins, almonds, apples, and chia seeds and stir well.
2. Grease your Slow cooker with the spray, line it with parchment paper, spread quinoa mix, cover, and cook on Low for 4 hours.
3. Leave mix aside to cool down, slice, and serve for breakfast.

per serving: 145 calories,3.7g protein, 18g carbohydrates, 7.4g fat, 1.5g fiber, 41mg cholesterol, 36mg sodium, 177mg potassium.

Raspberry Bowls

Preparation time: 10 minutes
Cooking time: 8 hours
Servings: 4

Ingredients:

- 2 cups of water
- 1 tablespoon olive oil
- 1 cup steel-cut oats
- 1 tablespoon liquid honey
- 1 cup organic almond milk
- ½ teaspoon vanilla extract
- 1 cup raspberries
- 4 tablespoons walnuts, chopped

Directions:

1. In your Slow cooker, mix oil with water, oats, honey, milk, vanilla, and raspberries, cover, and cook on Low for 8 hours.
2. Stir oatmeal, divide into bowls, sprinkle walnuts on top, and serve for breakfast.

per serving: 291 calories,5.1g protein, 19.2g carbohydrates, 23.5g fat, 4.9g fiber, 0mg cholesterol, 16mg sodium, 291mg potassium.

Flaxseeds Oats

Preparation time: 10 minutes
Cooking time: 8 hours
Servings: 4

Ingredients:

- 1 cup steel-cut oats
- 2 cups organic almond milk
- 2 tablespoons honey
- 2 teaspoons cinnamon powder
- 2 cups of water
- 2 teaspoons flaxseed
- Cooking spray
- 2 tablespoons blackberries
- 1 teaspoon vanilla extract

Directions:

1. Grease your Slow cooker with the cooking spray and add oats, vanilla extract, almond milk, maple syrup, cinnamon, water, and flaxseed, cover and cook on Low for 8 hours. Stir oats, divide into bowls, sprinkle blackberries on top, and serve for breakfast.

per serving: 357 calories,4.3g protein, 23g carbohydrates, 29.5g fat, 3.9g fiber, 0mg cholesterol, 25mg sodium, 373mg potassium.

Butternut Squash Bowls

Preparation time: 10 minutes
Cooking time: 8 hours
Servings: 6

Ingredients:

- ½ cup almonds, soaked for 12 hours in the water and drained
- ½ cup walnuts, chopped
- 2 apples, peeled, cored, and cubed
- 1 butternut squash, peeled and cubed
- ½ teaspoon nutmeg, ground
- 1 teaspoon cinnamon powder
- 1 tablespoon liquid honey
- 1 cup organic almond milk

Directions:

1. In your Slow cooker, mix almonds with walnuts, apples, squash, nutmeg, cinnamon, honey, and milk, cover, and cook on Low for 8 hours.
2. Stir oatmeal, divide into bowls, and serve.

per serving: 181 calories,4.8g protein, 20g carbohydrates, 10.8g fat, 4.2g fiber, 0mg cholesterol, 27mg sodium, 307mg potassium.

Breakfast Granola

Preparation time: 10 minutes
Cooking time: 2 hours
Servings: 8

Ingredients:

- 5 cups old-fashioned rolled oats
- 1/3 cup olive oil
- 2 tablespoons of liquid honey
- ½ cup almonds, chopped
- 1 tablespoon vanilla
- 2 teaspoons cinnamon powder
- 1 cup raisins
- Cooking spray

Directions:

1. Grease your Slow cooker with cooking spray, add oats, oil, honey, almonds, vanilla, raisins, and cinnamon, toss just a bit, cover, and cook on High for 2 hours, stirring every 30 minutes.
2. Divide into bowls and serve for breakfast.

per serving: 181 calories,1.8g protein, 20.2g carbohydrates, 11.5g fat, 1.4g fiber, 0mg cholesterol, 2mg sodium, 184mg potassium.

Pecans and Pineapple Granola

Preparation time: 10 minutes
Cooking time: 1 hour and 30 minutes
Servings: 7

Ingredients:

- 1 cup almonds, sliced
- 4 cups old-fashioned oats
- ½ cup pecans, chopped
- ½ teaspoon ginger, ground
- ½ cup of olive oil
- ½ cup dried coconut
- ½ cup cherries
- ½ cup pineapple, dried

Directions:

1. In your Slow cooker, mix oil with almonds, oats, pecans, ginger, coconut, cherries, and pineapple, toss, cover, cook on High for 1 hour and 30 minutes, stir again, divide into bowls and serve for breakfast.

per serving: 507 calories,10.6g protein, 47.4g carbohydrates, 33.3g fat, 8.4g fiber, 0mg cholesterol, 6mg sodium, 425mg potassium.

Creamy Oatmeal

Preparation time: 10 minutes
Cooking time: 8 hours
Servings: 8

Ingredients:

- 6 cups of water
- 2 cups organic almond milk
- 2 cups steel-cut oats
- 1 cup Greek yogurt
- 1 teaspoon cinnamon powder
- 2 cups strawberries, halved
- 1 teaspoon vanilla extract

Directions:

1. In your Slow cooker, mix water with milk, oats, yogurt, cinnamon, strawberries, and vanilla, toss, cover, and cook on Low for 8 hours.
2. Divide into bowls and serve for breakfast.

per serving: 211 calories,5.6g protein, 14.2g carbohydrates, 15.8g fat, 3g fiber, 1mg cholesterol, 25mg sodium, 292mg potassium.

Honey and Carrot Oatmeal

Preparation time: 10 minutes
Cooking time: 8 hours
Servings: 2

Ingredients:

- ½ cup old fashioned oats
- 1 cup organic almond milk
- 2 carrots, peeled and grated
- ½ teaspoon cinnamon powder
- 1 teaspoon liquid honey
- ¼ cup walnuts, chopped
- Cooking spray

Directions:

1. Grease your slow cooker with cooking spray, add the oats, milk, carrots, and the other ingredients, toss, put the lid on and cook on Low for 8 hours.
2. Divide the oatmeal into 2 bowls and serve.

per serving: 564 calories,12g protein, 43.9g carbohydrates, 40.4g fat, 9.1g fiber, 0mg cholesterol, 60mg sodium, 776mg potassium.

Vegetable Recipes

Aromatic Wild Rice Pilaf

Preparation time: 10 minutes
Cooking time: 7 hours
Servings: 12

Ingredients:

- ½ cup wild rice
- ½ cup barley
- 2/3 cup wheat berries
- 27 ounces vegetable stock
- 2 cups baby lima beans
- 1 red bell pepper, chopped
- 1 yellow onion, chopped
- 1 tablespoon olive oil
- 1 teaspoon sage, dried and crushed
- 4 garlic cloves, minced

Directions:

1. In your Slow cooker, mix rice with barley, wheat berries, lima beans, bell pepper, onion, oil, sage, and garlic, stir, cover, and cook on Low for 7 hours.
2. Stir one more time, divide between plates and serve as a side dish.

per serving: 115 calories,4.7g protein, 21g carbohydrates, 1.8g fat, 3.8g fiber, 0mg cholesterol, 37mg sodium, 231mg potassium.

Apples and Potatoes Bowls

Preparation time: 10 minutes
Cooking time: 7 hours
Servings: 10

Ingredients:

- 2 green apples, cored and cut into wedges
- 3 pounds sweet potatoes, peeled and cut into medium wedges
- 1 cup coconut cream
- 1 cup apple butter
- 1 and ½ teaspoon pumpkin pie spice

Directions:

1. In your Slow cooker, mix sweet potatoes with green apples, cream, apple butter, and spice, toss, cover, and cook on Low for 7 hours.
2. Toss, divide between plates, and serve as a side dish.

per serving: 288 calories,2.9g protein, 57.4g carbohydrates, 6.1g fat, 7.6g fiber, 0mg cholesterol, 20mg sodium, 1247mg potassium.

Classic Mix

Preparation time: 10 minutes
Cooking time: 3 hours
Servings: 4

Ingredients:

- 1 and ½ cups red onion, cut into medium chunks
- 1 cup cherry tomatoes, halved
- 2 and ½ cups zucchini, sliced
- 2 cups yellow bell pepper, chopped
- 1 cup mushrooms, sliced
- 2 tablespoons basil, chopped
- 1 tablespoon thyme, chopped
- ½ cup olive oil
- ½ cup balsamic vinegar

Directions:

1. In your Slow cooker, mix onion pieces with tomatoes, zucchini, bell pepper, mushrooms, basil, thyme, oil, and vinegar, toss to coat everything, cover, and cook on High for 3 hours.
2. Divide between plates and serve as a side dish.

per serving: 295 calories,3.8g protein, 16.3g carbohydrates, 25.8g fat, 4.3g fiber, 0mg cholesterol, 22mg sodium, 739mg potassium.

Okra Saute

Preparation time: 10 minutes
Cooking time: 3 hours
Servings: 4

Ingredients:

- 2 cups okra, sliced
- 1 and ½ cups red onion, roughly chopped
- 1 cup cherry tomatoes, halved
- 2 ½ cups zucchini, sliced
- 2 cups bell peppers, sliced
- 1 cup white mushrooms, sliced
- ½ cup olive oil
- ½ cup balsamic vinegar
- 2 tablespoons basil, chopped
- 1 tablespoon thyme

Directions:

1. In your Slow cooker, mix okra with onion, tomatoes, zucchini, bell peppers, mushrooms, basil, and thyme. In a bowl mix oil with vinegar, whisk well, add to the slow cooker, cover and cook on High for 3 hours. Divide between plates and serve as a side dish.

per serving: 304 calories,3.9g protein, 17.7g carbohydrates, 25.8g fat, 5.1g fiber, 0mg cholesterol, 19mg sodium, 703mg potassium.

Corn Mix

Preparation time: 10 minutes
Cooking time: 8 hours
Servings: 4

Ingredients:

- 3 garlic cloves, minced
- 1 small green bell pepper, chopped
- 1 small yellow onion, chopped
- 1 cup of water
- 16 ounces okra, sliced
- 2 cups corn kernels
- 1 and ½ teaspoon smoked paprika
- 28 ounces canned tomatoes, crushed
- 1 teaspoon oregano, dried
- 1 teaspoon thyme, dried
- 1 teaspoon marjoram, dried
- A pinch of cayenne pepper

Directions:

1. In your Slow cooker, mix garlic with bell pepper, onion, water, okra, corn, paprika, tomatoes, oregano, thyme, marjoram, cayenne, cover, cook on Low for 8 hours, divide between plates and serve as a side dish.

per serving: 171 calories, 7.3g protein, 36.2g carbohydrates, 1.8g fat, 9.6g fiber, 0mg cholesterol, 33mg sodium, 1138mg potassium.

Beets Salad

Preparation time: 10 minutes
Cooking time: 7 hours
Servings: 12

Ingredients:

- 5 beets, peeled and sliced
- ¼ cup balsamic vinegar
- 1/3 cup honey
- 1 tablespoon rosemary, chopped
- 2 tablespoons olive oil
- 2 garlic cloves, minced

Directions:

1. In your Slow cooker, mix beets with vinegar, honey, oil, rosemary, and garlic, cover, and cook on Low for 7 hours.
2. Divide between plates and serve as a side dish.

per serving: 70 calories, 0.8g protein, 12.3g carbohydrates, 2.5g fat, 1g fiber, 0mg cholesterol, 33mg sodium, 140mg potassium.

Cauliflower Gratin

Preparation time: 10 minutes
Cooking time: 7 hours
Servings: 12

Ingredients:
- 16 ounces baby carrots
- 6 tablespoons pumpkin puree
- 1 cauliflower head, florets separated
- 1 yellow onion, chopped
- 1 teaspoon mustard powder
- 1 ½ cups coconut milk
- 6 ounces tofu, crumbled

Directions:
1. Put the pumpkin puree in your Slow cooker, add carrots, cauliflower, onion, mustard powder, and coconut milk, and toss.
2. Sprinkle tofu all over, cover, and cook on Low for 7 hours.
3. Divide between plates and serve as a side dish.

per serving: 105 calories, 2.8g protein, 7.8g carbohydrates, 7.9g fat, 2.9g fiber, 0mg cholesterol, 43mg sodium, 287mg potassium.

Summer Squash Bowls

Preparation time: 10 minutes
Cooking time: 2 hours
Servings: 4

Ingredients:
- ¼ cup olive oil
- 2 tablespoons basil, chopped
- 2 tablespoons balsamic vinegar
- 2 garlic cloves, minced
- 2 teaspoons mustard
- 3 summer squash, sliced
- 2 zucchinis, sliced

Directions:
1. In your Slow cooker, mix squash with zucchinis, mustard, garlic, vinegar, basil, and oil, toss a bit, cover, and cook on High for 2 hours.
2. Divide between plates and serve as a side dish.

per serving: 154 calories, 2.7g protein, 8.2g carbohydrates, 13.5g fat, 2.4g fiber, 0mg cholesterol, 13mg sodium, 495mg potassium.

Basil Side Salad

Preparation time: 10 minutes
Cooking time: 2 hours
Servings: 4

Ingredients:
- 2 garlic cloves, minced
- ½ cup olive oil
- ¼ cup basil, chopped
- 1 red bell pepper, chopped
- 1 eggplant, roughly chopped
- 1 summer squash, cubed
- 1 Vidalia onion, cut into wedges
- 1 zucchini, sliced
- 1 green bell pepper, chopped

Directions:
1. In your Slow cooker, mix red bell pepper with green one, squash, zucchini, eggplant, onion, basil, oil, and garlic, toss gently, cover, and cook on High for 2 hours.
2. Divide between plates and serve as a side dish.

per serving: 282 calories,2.8g protein, 15g carbohydrates, 25.7g fat, 6g fiber, 0mg cholesterol, 10mg sodium, 568mg potassium.

Italian Squash Mix

Preparation time: 10 minutes
Cooking time: 1 hour and 30 minutes
Servings: 4

Ingredients:
- 12 small squash, peeled and cut into wedges
- 2 red bell peppers, cut into wedges
- 2 green bell peppers, cut into wedges
- 1/3 cup Italian dressing
- 1 red onion, cut into wedges
- 1 tablespoon parsley, chopped

Directions:
1. In your Slow cooker, mix squash with red bell peppers, green bell peppers, and Italian dressing, cover, and cook on High for 1 hour and 30 minutes.
2. Add parsley, toss, divide between plates and serve as a side dish.

per serving: 144 calories,5.3g protein, 21g carbohydrates, 6.4g fat, 5.3g fiber, 13mg cholesterol, 44mg sodium, 1094mg potassium.

Blueberry Salad

Preparation time: 10 minutes
Cooking time: 1 hour
Servings: 3

Ingredients:

- ¼ cup pecans, chopped
- ½ teaspoon honey
- 2 teaspoons maple syrup
- 1 tablespoon white vinegar
- 2 tablespoons orange juice
- 1 tablespoon olive oil
- 4 cups spinach
- 2 oranges, peeled and cut into segments
- 1 cup blueberries

Directions:

1. In your Slow cooker, mix pecans with honey, maple syrup, vinegar, orange juice, oil, spinach, oranges, and blueberries, toss, cover, and cook on High for 1 hour.
2. Divide between plates and serve as a side dish.

per serving: 253 calories, 4.2g protein, 29.9g carbohydrates, 15.2g fat, 6.5g fiber, 0mg cholesterol, 33mg sodium, 574mg potassium.

Rice Mix

Preparation time: 6 minutes
Cooking time: 5 hours
Servings: 4

Ingredients:

- 2 cups brown rice
- 1 cup mixed carrots, peas, corn, and green beans
- 2 cups of water
- ½ teaspoon green chili
- ½ teaspoon ginger, grated
- 3 garlic cloves, minced
- 2 tablespoons pumpkin puree
- 1 cinnamon stick
- 1 tablespoon cumin seeds
- 2 bay leaves
- 3 whole cloves
- 5 black peppercorns
- 2 whole cardamoms
- 1 tablespoon honey

Directions:

1. Put the water in your Slow cooker, add rice, mixed veggies, green chili, grated ginger, garlic, cinnamon stick, whole cloves, pumpkin puree, cumin seeds, bay leaves, cardamoms, black peppercorns, and honey, stir, cover, and cook on Low for 5 hours.
2. Discard the cinnamon, divide between plates and serve as a side dish.

per serving: 388 calories, 8.2g protein, 81.7g carbohydrates, 2.9g fat, 3.7g fiber, 0mg cholesterol, 19mg sodium, 315mg potassium.

Farro and Cherries

Preparation time: 10 minutes
Cooking time: 5 hours
Servings: 6

Ingredients:
- 1 tablespoon apple cider vinegar
- 1 cup whole-grain farro
- 1 teaspoon lemon juice
- 3 cups of water
- 1 tablespoon olive oil
- ¼ cup green onions, chopped
- 10 mint leaves, chopped
- 2 cups cherries, pitted and halved

Directions:
1. Put the water in your Slow cooker, add farro, stir, cover, cook on Low for 5 hours, drain and transfer to a bowl.
2. Add oil, lemon juice, vinegar, fresh cherries, green onions, and mint, toss, divide between plates and serve as a side dish.

per serving: 124 calories,3.4g protein, 20.6g carbohydrates, 3.7g fat, 3.1g fiber, 0mg cholesterol, 14mg sodium, 103mg potassium.

Cilantro Rice

Preparation time: 10 minutes
Cooking time: 4 hours
Servings: 8

Ingredients:
- 1 cup of brown rice
- 1 and ¼ cups vegetable stock
- ½ cup cilantro, chopped
- ½ avocado, pitted, peeled, and chopped
- ¼ cup hot red pepper sauce

Directions:
1. Put the rice in your Slow cooker, add the stock, stir, cover, cook on Low for 4 hours, fluff with a fork, and transfer to a bowl.
2. In your food processor, mix avocado with hot sauce and cilantro, blend well, pour over rice, toss well, divide between plates, and serve as a side dish.

per serving: 120 calories,2.1g protein, 20.9g carbohydrates, 3.1g fat, 1.8g fiber, 0mg cholesterol, 62mg sodium, 130mg potassium.

Black Beans and Cumin Mix

Preparation time: 10 minutes
Cooking time: 7 hours
Servings: 8

Ingredients:

- 1 cup black beans, soaked overnight, drained, and rinsed
- 1 cup of water
- 1 spring onion, chopped
- 2 garlic cloves, minced
- ½ teaspoon cumin seeds

Directions:

1. In your Slow cooker, mix beans with water, onion, garlic, and cumin seeds, stir, cover, and cook on Low for 7 hours.
2. Divide everything between plates and serve as a side dish.

per serving: 85 calories,5.3g protein, 15.6g carbohydrates, 0.4g fat, 3.8g fiber, 0mg cholesterol, 3mg sodium, 370mg potassium.

Oregano Eggplant

Preparation time: 10 minutes
Cooking time: 2 hours
Servings: 2

Ingredients:

- 2 small eggplants, roughly cubed
- ½ cup Greek-style yogurt
- 1 tablespoon olive oil
- A pinch of hot pepper flakes
- 2 tablespoons oregano, chopped

Directions:

1. In your slow cooker, mix the eggplants with the yogurt and the other ingredients, toss, put the lid on and cook on High for 2 hours.
2. Divide between plates and serve as a side dish.

per serving: 281 calories,8.1g protein, 38.9g carbohydrates, 13.4g fat, 21.3g fiber, 20mg cholesterol, 37mg sodium, 1424mg potassium.

Thyme Okra Mix

Preparation time: 10 minutes
Cooking time: 2 hours
Servings: 4

Ingredients:

- 2 cups okra, sliced
- 1 cup cherry tomatoes, halved
- 1 tablespoon olive oil
- ½ teaspoon turmeric powder
- 2 tablespoons balsamic vinegar
- 2 tablespoons basil, chopped
- 1 tablespoon thyme, chopped

Directions:

2. In your slow cooker, mix the okra with the tomatoes, and the other ingredients, toss, put the lid on and cook on High for 2 hours.
3. Divide between plates and serve as a side dish.

per serving: 63 calories,1.5g protein, 6.2g carbohydrates, 3.8g fat, 2.5g fiber, 0mg cholesterol, 7mg sodium, 278mg potassium.

Cabbage Mix

Preparation time: 10 minutes
Cooking time: 2 hours
Servings: 2

Ingredients:

- 1 red onion, sliced
- 1 cup green cabbage, shredded
- 1 cup baby kale
- ½ cup canned tomatoes, crushed
- ½ teaspoon hot paprika
- ½ teaspoon Italian seasoning
- 1 tablespoon dill, chopped

Directions:

1. In your slow cooker, mix the cabbage with the kale, onion, and the other ingredients, toss, put the lid on and cook on High for 2 hours.
2. Divide between plates and serve right away as a side dish.

per serving: 69 calories,3.3g protein, 14.4g carbohydrates, 0.9g fat, 3.8g fiber, 1mg cholesterol, 32mg sodium, 298mg potassium.

Thyme Corn Mix

Preparation time: 10 minutes
Cooking time: 4 hours
Servings: 2

Ingredients:

- 4 garlic cloves, minced
- 1 tablespoon olive oil
- 1 pound white mushroom caps, halved
- 1 cup of corn kernels
- 1 cup canned tomatoes, crushed
- ¼ teaspoon thyme, dried
- ½ cup vegetable stock
- 2 tablespoons parsley, chopped

Directions:

1. Grease your slow cooker with the oil, and mix the garlic with the mushrooms, corn, and the other ingredients inside.
2. Toss, put the lid on, and cook on Low for 4 hours.
3. Divide between plates and serve as a side dish.

per serving: 168 calories, 5.5g protein, 22.8g carbohydrates, 8.2g fat, 4.2g fiber, 0mg cholesterol, 62mg sodium, 650mg potassium.

Italian Style Mix

Preparation time: 10 minutes
Cooking time: 5 hours
Servings: 4

Ingredients:

- 2 tablespoons tomato paste
- 2 cups black beans
- ¼ cup vegetable stock
- 1 red onion, sliced
- Cooking spray
- 1 teaspoon Italian seasoning
- ½ celery rib, chopped
- ½ red bell pepper, chopped
- ½ sweet red pepper, chopped
- ¼ teaspoon mustard seeds
- 1 tablespoon cilantro, chopped

Directions:

1. Grease the slow cooker with the cooking spray, and mix the beans with the stock, onion, and the other ingredients inside.
2. Put the lid on, cook on Low for 5 hours, divide between plates, and serve as a side dish.

per serving: 360 calories, 21.9g protein, 66.3g carbohydrates, 1.9g fat, 16g fiber, 66.3mg cholesterol, 27mg sodium, 182mg potassium.

Hot Mix

Preparation time: 10 minutes
Cooking time: 2 hours
Servings: 2

Ingredients:
- ¼ cup carrots, grated
- 1 pound zucchinis, roughly cubed
- 1 teaspoon hot paprika
- ½ teaspoon chili powder
- 2 spring onions, chopped
- ½ tablespoon olive oil
- ½ teaspoon curry powder
- 1 garlic clove, minced
- ½ teaspoon ginger powder
- 1 tablespoon cilantro, chopped

Directions:
1. In your slow cooker, mix the carrots with the zucchinis, paprika, and the other ingredients, toss, put the lid on and cook on Low for 2 hours.
2. Divide between plates and serve as a side dish.

per serving: 84 calories,3.4g protein, 11.5g carbohydrates, 4.2g fat, 3.7g fiber, 0mg cholesterol, 42mg sodium, 714mg potassium.

Creamy Sweet Potatoes

Preparation time: 10 minutes
Cooking time: 4 hours
Servings: 2

Ingredients:
- ½ pound sweet potatoes, halved and sliced
- 2 scallions, chopped
- 1 tablespoon avocado oil
- 2 ounces of coconut milk
- ¼ cup vegetable stock
- 1 tablespoons parsley, chopped

Directions:
1. In your slow cooker, mix the potatoes with the scallions and the other ingredients, toss, put the lid on and cook on High for 4 hours.
2. Divide the mix between plates and serve.

per serving: 216 calories,2.9g protein, 35.3g carbohydrates, 7.9g fat, 6.2g fiber, 0mg cholesterol, 36mg sodium, 1090mg potassium.

Aromatic Sweet Potatoes

Preparation time: 10 minutes
Cooking time: 3 hours
Servings: 2

Ingredients:
- ½ pound sweet potatoes, thinly sliced
- 1 tablespoon sage, chopped
- 2 tablespoons orange juice
- ½ cup vegetable stock
- ½ tablespoon olive oil

Directions:
1. In your slow cooker, mix the potatoes with the sage and the other ingredients, toss, put the lid on and cook on High for 3 hours.
2. Divide between plates and serve as a side dish.

per serving: 175 calories,2.1g protein, 34.1g carbohydrates, 3.9g fat, 5.2g fiber, 0mg cholesterol, 23mg sodium, 967mg potassium.

Vegetables and Almonds Mix

Preparation time: 10 minutes
Cooking time: 3 hours
Servings: 2

Ingredients:
- 2 cups cauliflower florets
- 2 ounces tomato paste
- 1 small yellow onion, chopped
- 1 tablespoon chives, chopped
- 1 tablespoon almonds, sliced

Directions:
1. In your slow cooker, mix the cauliflower with the tomato paste and the other ingredients, toss, put the lid on and cook on High for 3 hours.
2. Divide between plates and serve as a side dish.

per serving: 80 calories,4.3g protein, 14.6g carbohydrates, 1.8g fat, 4.8g fiber, 0mg cholesterol, 59mg sodium, 668mg potassium.

Sweet Brussels Sprouts

Preparation time: 10 minutes
Cooking time: 3 hours
Servings: 2

Ingredients:

- ½ pounds Brussels sprouts, trimmed and halved
- 2 tablespoons mustard
- ½ cup vegetable stock
- 1 tablespoon olive oil
- 2 tablespoons maple syrup
- 1 tablespoon thyme, chopped

Directions:

1. In your slow cooker, mix the sprouts with the mustard and the other ingredients, toss, put the lid on and cook on Low for 3 hours.
2. Divide between plates and serve as a side dish.

per serving: 219 calories,6.9g protein, 28.7g carbohydrates, 10.8g fat, 6.5g fiber, 0mg cholesterol, 44mg sodium, 569mg potassium.

Nuts Black Beans Mix

Preparation time: 10 minutes
Cooking time: 6 hours
Servings: 2

Ingredients:

- ½ pound black beans, soaked overnight and drained
- ½ cup vegetable stock
- ½ tablespoon lime juice
- 2 tablespoons cilantro, chopped
- 2 tablespoons pine nuts

Directions:

1. In your slow cooker, mix the beans with the stock and the other ingredients, toss, put the lid on and cook on Low for 6 hours.
2. Divide everything between plates and serve.

per serving: 446 calories,25.8g protein, 72.1g carbohydrates, 7.5g fat, 17.7g fiber, 0mg cholesterol, 19mg sodium, 1738mg potassium.

Onion Broccoli Mix

Preparation time: 10 minutes
Cooking time: 2 hours
Servings: 10

Ingredients:

- 6 cups broccoli florets
- 1 and ½ cups cheddar cheese, shredded
- 1 cup coconut cream
- ½ teaspoon Worcestershire sauce
- ¼ cup yellow onion, chopped
- 2 tablespoons olive oil

Directions:

1. In a bowl, mix broccoli with coconut cream, cheese, onion, and Worcestershire sauce, toss and transfer to your Slow cooker. Add olive oil, toss again, cover, and cook on High for 2 hours. Serve as a side dish.

per serving: 120 calories,3.5g protein, 5.4g carbohydrates, 10.4g fat, 2g fiber, 0mg cholesterol, 24mg sodium, 240mg potassium.

Tender Bean Medley

Preparation time: 10 minutes
Cooking time: 5 hours
Servings: 12

Ingredients:

- 2 celery ribs, chopped
- 1 green bell pepper, chopped
- 1 yellow onion, chopped
- 1 sweet red pepper, chopped
- ½ cup honey
- ½ cup Italian dressing
- ½ cup of water
- 1 tablespoon cider vinegar
- 2 bay leaves
- 16 ounces kidney beans, drained
- 15 ounces canned black-eyed peas, drained
- 15 ounces canned northern beans, drained
- 15 ounces canned corn, drained
- 15 ounces canned lima beans, drained
- 15 ounces canned black beans, drained

Directions:

1. In your Slow cooker, mix celery with red and green bell pepper, onion, honey, Italian dressing, water, vinegar, bay leaves, kidney beans, black-eyed peas, northern beans, corn, lima beans, and black beans, stir, cover, and cook on Low for 5 hours. Divide between plates and serve as a side dish.

per serving: 559 calories,26.9g protein, 107.8g carbohydrates, 6.6g fat, 19.8g fiber, 7mg cholesterol, 55mg sodium, 1849mg potassium.

Honey Green Beans Mix

Preparation time: 10 minutes
Cooking time: 2 hours
Servings: 12

Ingredients:
- 16 ounces green beans
- ½ cup honey
- ½ cup olive oil
- ¾ teaspoon soy sauce, low sodium

Directions:
1. In your Slow cooker, mix green beans with honey, olive oil, soy sauce, stir, cover, and cook on Low for 2 hours.
2. Divide between plates and serve as a side dish.

per serving: 127 calories,0.8g protein, 14.4g carbohydrates, 8.5g fat, 1.3g fiber, 0mg cholesterol, 21mg sodium, 87mg potassium.

Green Onions with Creamy Chicken

Preparation time: 10 minutes
Cooking time: 4 hours
Servings: 20

Ingredients:
- 1 cup organic almond milk
- 3 tablespoons olive oil
- 2 cups coconut cream
- ¼ cup honey
- 2 cups chicken fillet, minced
- 2 tablespoons green onions, chopped

Directions:
1. In your Slow cooker, mix all ingredients and cook on Low for 4 hours.
2. Stir the cooked meal, divide between plates and serve as a side dish.

per serving: 116 calories,4.7g protein, 5.3g carbohydrates, 9g fat, 0.6g fiber, 12mg cholesterol, 23mg sodium, 101mg potassium.

Marjoram Peas and Carrots

Preparation time: 10 minutes
Cooking time: 5 hours
Servings: 12

Ingredients:
- 1 yellow onion, chopped
- 1 pound carrots, sliced
- 16 ounces peas
- ¼ cup olive oil
- ¼ cup of water
- ¼ cup honey
- 4 garlic cloves, minced
- 1 teaspoon marjoram, dried

Directions:
1. In your Slow cooker, mix the onion with carrots, peas, olive oil, water, honey, garlic, and marjoram, cover, and cook on Low for 5 hours.
2. Stir peas and carrots mix, divide between plates and serve as a side dish.

per serving: 109 calories, 2.6g protein, 16.2g carbohydrates, 4.4g fat, 3.1g fiber, 0mg cholesterol, 29mg sodium, 235mg potassium.

Garlic Cauliflower Pilaf

Preparation time: 10 minutes
Cooking time: 3 hours
Servings: 6

Ingredients:
- 1 cup cauliflower rice
- 6 green onions, chopped
- 3 tablespoons ghee, melted
- 2 garlic cloves, minced
- ½ pound Portobello mushrooms, sliced
- 2 cups warm water

Directions:
1. In your Slow cooker, mix cauliflower rice with green onions, melted ghee, garlic, mushrooms, water, stir well, cover, and cook on Low for 3 hours.
2. Divide between plates and serve as a side dish.

per serving: 80 calories, 1.8g protein, 3.4g carbohydrates, 6.7g fat, 0.4g fiber, 16mg cholesterol, 25mg sodium, 155mg potassium.

Squash Salad

Preparation time: 10 minutes
Cooking time: 4 hours
Servings: 8

Ingredients:

- 1 tablespoon olive oil
- 1 cup carrots, chopped
- 1 yellow onion, chopped
- 1 teaspoon honey
- 1 and ½ teaspoons curry powder
- 1 garlic clove, minced
- 1 big butternut squash, peeled and cubed
- ¼ teaspoon ginger, grated
- ½ teaspoon cinnamon powder
- 3 cups of coconut milk

Directions:

1. In your Slow cooker, mix oil with carrots, onion, honey, curry powder, garlic, squash, ginger, cinnamon, and coconut milk, stir well, cover, and cook on Low for 4 hours.
2. Stir, divide between plates, and serve as a side dish.

per serving: 246 calories,2.6g protein, 10.8g carbohydrates, 23.3g fat, 3.1g fiber, 0mg cholesterol, 25mg sodium, 371mg potassium.

Spinach Salad

Preparation time: 10 minutes
Cooking time: 4 hours
Servings: 12

Ingredients:

- 3 pounds butternut squash, peeled and cubed
- 1 yellow onion, chopped
- 2 teaspoons thyme, chopped
- 3 garlic cloves, minced
- 10 ounces vegetable stock
- 6 ounces baby spinach

Directions:

1. In your Slow cooker, mix squash cubes with onion, thyme, and stock, stir, cover, and cook on Low for 4 hours.
2. Transfer squash mixture to a bowl, add spinach, toss, divide between plates and serve as a side dish.

per serving: 61 calories,1.8g protein, 15.2g carbohydrates, 0.2g fat, 3g fiber, 0mg cholesterol, 28mg sodium, 496mg potassium.

Italian Style Mushrooms

Preparation time: 10 minutes
Cooking time: 4 hours
Servings: 6

Ingredients:
- 1 yellow onion, chopped
- 1 pounds mushrooms, halved
- 2 tablespoons olive oil
- 1 teaspoon Italian seasoning
- 1 teaspoon sweet paprika

Directions:
1. In your Slow cooker, mix mushrooms with onion, olive oil, Italian seasoning, and paprika, toss, cover, and cook on Low for 4 hours.
2. Divide between plates and serve as a side dish.

per serving: 67 calories, 2.6g protein, 4.5g carbohydrates, 5.2g fat, 1.3g fiber, 1mg cholesterol, 5mg sodium, 276mg potassium.

Apple Juice and Sweet Potatoes

Preparation time: 10 minutes
Cooking time: 5 hours
Servings: 10

Ingredients:
- 8 sweet potatoes, halved and sliced
- 1 cup walnuts, chopped
- ½ cup cherries, dried and chopped
- 2 tablespoons honey
- ¼ cup apple juice

Directions:
1. Arrange sweet potatoes in your slow cooker, add walnuts, dried cherries, honey, apple juice, and toss a bit, cover, and cook on Low for 5 hours.
2. Divide between plates and serve as a side dish.

per serving: 150 calories, 3.7g protein, 19g carbohydrates, 7.5g fat, 2.7g fiber, 0mg cholesterol, 5mg sodium, 445mg potassium.

Chipotle Sweet Potatoes

Preparation time: 10 minutes
Cooking time: 4 hours
Servings: 10

Ingredients:

- 1 sweet onion, chopped
- 2 tablespoons olive oil
- ¼ cup parsley, chopped
- 2 shallots, chopped
- 2 teaspoons chipotle pepper, crushed
- 4 big sweet potatoes, shredded
- 8 ounces coconut cream
- ½ teaspoon sweet paprika
- Cooking spray

Directions:

1. Heat a pan with the oil over medium-high heat, add shallots and onion, stir, cook for 6 minutes and transfer to a bowl.
2. Add parsley, chipotle pepper, sweet potatoes, coconut cream, paprika, and stir, pour everything in your Slow cooker after you've greased it with some cooking spray, cover, cook on Low for 4 hours, leave aside to cool down a bit, divide between plates and serve as a side dish.

per serving: 119 calories,1.2g protein, 11.2g carbohydrates, 8.3g fat, 2.1g fiber, 0mg cholesterol, 8mg sodium, 340mg potassium.

Sweet Potato Puree with Allspices

Preparation time: 10 minutes
Cooking time: 5 hours
Servings: 6

Ingredients:

- 2 pounds sweet potatoes, peeled and sliced
- 1 tablespoon cinnamon powder
- 1 cup apple juice
- 1 teaspoon nutmeg, ground
- ¼ teaspoon cloves, ground
- ½ teaspoon allspices
- 1 tablespoon olive oil

Directions:

1. In your Slow cooker, mix sweet potatoes with cinnamon, apple juice, nutmeg, cloves, and allspice, stir, cover, and cook on Low for 5 hours.
2. Mash using a potato masher, add olive oil, whisk well, divide between plates and serve as a side dish.

per serving: 220 calories,2.4g protein, 47.2g carbohydrates, 2.8g fat, 6.4g fiber, 0mg cholesterol, 16mg sodium, 129mg potassium.

Garlic Cauliflower Puree

Preparation time: 10 minutes
Cooking time: 5 hours
Servings: 6

Ingredients:
- 1 cauliflower head, florets separated
- 1/3 cup dill, chopped
- 6 garlic cloves
- 2 tablespoons olive oil

Directions:
1. Put cauliflower in your Slow cooker, add dill, garlic, and water to cover cauliflower, cover, and cook on High for 5 hours.
2. Drain cauliflower and dill, add and olive oil, mash using a potato masher, whisk well and serve as a side dish.

per serving: 62 calories,1.6g protein, 4.8g carbohydrates, 4.9g fat, 1.5g fiber, 0mg cholesterol, 19mg sodium, 234mg potassium.

Easy Cabbage Mix

Preparation time: 10 minutes
Cooking time: 6 hours
Servings: 4

Ingredients:
- 1-pound red cabbage, shredded
- 1 apple, peeled, cored, and roughly chopped
- ¼ cup chicken stock, low sodium
- ½ tablespoon olive oil

Directions:
1. In your slow cooker, mix the cabbage with the apple and the other ingredients, toss, put the lid on and cook on Low for 6 hours.
2. Divide between plates and serve as a side dish.

per serving: 73 calories,1.6g protein, 14.3g carbohydrates, 2g fat, 4.2g fiber, 0mg cholesterol, 69mg sodium, 253mg potassium.

Fish and Seafood

Chili Tuna

Preparation time: 10 minutes
Cooking time: 2 hours
Servings: 6

Ingredients:

- 1-pound tuna fillets, boneless and cubed
- ½ teaspoon red pepper flakes, crushed
- ¼ teaspoon cayenne pepper
- ½ cup chicken stock
- ½ teaspoon chili powder
- 1 tablespoon olive oil
- 1 tablespoon chives, chopped

Directions:

1. In your slow cooker, mix the tuna with the pepper flakes, cayenne, and the other ingredients, toss, put the lid on and cook on High for 2 hours.
2. Divide the tuna mix between plates and serve.

per serving: 297 calories,16g protein, 0.3g carbohydrates, 25.9g fat, 0.1g fiber, 0mg cholesterol, 66mg sodium, 10mg potassium.

Chives Tuna

Preparation time: 5 minutes
Cooking time: 2 hours
Servings: 5

Ingredients:

- 1-pound tuna fillets, boneless and roughly cubed
- 1 tablespoon ginger, grated
- 1 red onion, chopped
- 2 teaspoons olive oil
- Juice of 1 lime
- ¼ cup chicken stock
- 1 tablespoon chives, chopped

Directions:

1. In your slow cooker, mix the tuna with the ginger, onion, and the other ingredients, toss, put the lid on and cook on High for 2 hours.
2. Divide the mix into bowls and serve.

per serving: 363 calories,19.6g protein, 4.3g carbohydrates, 30.1g fat, 1g fiber, 0mg cholesterol, 40mg sodium, 63mg potassium.

Tuna with Vegetables

Preparation time: 10 minutes
Cooking time: 3 hours
Servings: 6

Ingredients:

- 1-pound tuna fillets, boneless
- 1 cup green beans, trimmed and halved
- ½ cup chicken stock
- ½ teaspoon sweet paprika
- ½ teaspoon garam masala
- 3 scallions, minced
- ½ teaspoon ginger, ground
- 1 tablespoon olive oil
- 1 tablespoon chives, chopped

Directions:

1. In your slow cooker, mix the tuna with the green beans, stock, and the other ingredients, toss gently, put the lid on, and cook on High for 3 hours.
2. Divide the mix between plates and serve.

per serving: 305 calories,16.5g protein, 2.2g carbohydrates, 25.9g fat, 0.9g fiber, 0mg cholesterol, 66mg sodium, 68mg potassium.

Tuna with Sweet Paprika and Vegetables

Preparation time: 5 minutes
Cooking time: 3 hours
Servings: 5

Ingredients:

- 1 pound tuna fillets, boneless
- ½ cup chicken stock
- 1 teaspoon sweet paprika
- ½ teaspoon chili powder
- 1 cup Brussels sprouts, trimmed and halved
- 1 red onion, chopped
- ½ teaspoon garlic powder
- 1 tablespoon cilantro, chopped

Directions:

1. In your slow cooker, mix the tuna with the stock, sprouts, and the other ingredients put the lid on, and cook on High for 3 hours.
2. Divide the mix between plates and serve.

per serving: 350 calories,20.1g protein, 4.3g carbohydrates, 28.4g fat, 1.4g fiber, 0mg cholesterol, 85mg sodium, 121mg potassium.

Fragrant Tuna

Preparation time: 5 minutes
Cooking time: 3 hours
Servings: 4

Ingredients:

- 1-pound tuna fillets, boneless and roughly cubed
- 1 tablespoon balsamic vinegar
- 3 garlic cloves, minced
- 1 tablespoon avocado oil
- ¼ cup chicken stock
- 1 tablespoon chives, chopped

Directions:

1. In your slow cooker, mix the tuna with the garlic, vinegar, and the other ingredients, toss, put the lid on and cook on Low for 3 hours.
2. Divide the mix into bowls and serve.

per serving: 421 calories,24.1g protein, 1.1g carbohydrates, 35.7g fat, 0.2g fiber, 0mg cholesterol, 48mg sodium, 26mg potassium.

Scallions Cod

Preparation time: 10 minutes
Cooking time: 3 hours
Servings: 2

Ingredients:

- 1 tablespoon olive oil
- 1-pound cod fillets, boneless
- 1 teaspoon sweet paprika
- ¼ cup chicken stock, low sodium
- 2 scallions, chopped
- ½ teaspoon rosemary, dried

Directions:

1. In your slow cooker, mix the cod with the paprika, oil, and the other ingredients, toss gently, put the lid on, and cook on High for 3 hours.
2. Divide everything between plates and serve.

per serving: 252 calories,41g protein, 2g carbohydrates, 9.3g fiber, 111mg cholesterol, 240mg sodium, 71mg potassium.

Chili Salmon Mix

Preparation time: 5 minutes
Cooking time: 3 hours
Servings: 2

Ingredients:
- 1-pound salmon fillets, boneless and roughly cubed
- 1 tablespoon coriander, chopped
- ½ teaspoon chili powder
- ¼ cup chicken stock, low sodium
- 3 scallions, chopped
- Juice of 1 lime
- 2 teaspoons avocado oil

Directions:
1. In your slow cooker, mix the salmon with the coriander, chili powder, and the other ingredients, toss gently, put the lid on, and cook on High for 3 hours.
2. Divide the mix between plates and serve.

per serving: 323 calories,44.7g protein, 4.3g carbohydrates, 14.9g fat, 1.1g fiber, 100mg cholesterol, 211mg sodium, 988mg potassium.

Coriander Cod

Preparation time: 5 minutes
Cooking time: 2 hours
Servings: 2

Ingredients:
- 1-pound cod fillets, boneless
- 3 scallions, chopped
- 2 teaspoons olive oil
- Juice of 1 lime
- 1 teaspoon coriander, ground
- 1 tablespoon parsley, chopped

Directions:
1. In your slow cooker, mix the cod with the scallions, the oil, and the other ingredients, rub gently, put the lid on and cook on High for 1 hour.
2. Divide everything between plates and serve.

per serving: 230 calories,41g protein, 1.8g carbohydrates, 6.8g fat, 0.7g fiber, 81mg cholesterol, 167mg sodium, 74mg potassium.

Cod and Tomatoes

Preparation time: 10 minutes
Cooking time: 3 hours
Servings: 2

Ingredients:
- 1-pound cod, boneless and roughly cubed
- 2 tablespoons basil pesto, low sodium
- 1 tablespoon olive oil
- 1 cup cherry tomatoes, halved
- 1 tablespoon chives, chopped
- ½ cup vegetable stock, low sodium

Directions:
1. In your slow cooker, mix the cod with the pesto, oil, and the other ingredients, toss, put the lid on and cook on High for 3 hours.
2. Divide the mix between plates and serve.

per serving: 317 calories, 52.8g protein, 3.9g carbohydrates, 9.2g fat, 1.3g fiber, 125mg cholesterol, 194mg sodium, 779mg potassium.

Turmeric Cod

Preparation time: 5 minutes
Cooking time: 3 hours
Servings: 2

Ingredients:
- 1-pound cod fillets, boneless
- Juice of 1 orange
- 1 tablespoon avocado oil
- 2 scallions, chopped
- ½ teaspoon turmeric powder
- ½ teaspoon sweet paprika

Directions:
1. In your slow cooker, mix the cod with the orange juice, oil, and the other ingredients, toss, put the lid on and cook on High for 3 hours.
2. Divide the mix between plates and serve.

per serving: 243 calories, 41.8g protein, 13g carbohydrates, 3.2g fat, 3.2g fiber, 81mg cholesterol, 165mg sodium, 256mg potassium.

Lemon and Garlic Cod

Preparation time: 10 minutes
Cooking time: 3 hours
Servings: 2

Ingredients:
- 1 tablespoon olive oil
- 1-pound cod fillets, boneless and cubed
- 1 tablespoon dill, chopped
- ½ teaspoon sweet paprika
- ½ teaspoon cumin, ground
- 2 garlic cloves, minced
- 1 teaspoon lemon juice
- 1 cup tomato passata

Directions:
1. In your slow cooker, mix the cod with the oil, dill, and the other ingredients, toss, put the lid on and cook on Low for 3 hours.
2. Divide the mix between plates and serve.

per serving: 270 calories,41.9g protein, 5.6g carbohydrates, 9.4g fat, 0.5g fiber, 111mg cholesterol, 147mg sodium, 88mg potassium.

Garam Masala Trout Mix

Preparation time: 10 minutes
Cooking time: 2 hours
Servings: 5

Ingredients:
- 1-pound trout fillets, boneless
- 1 tablespoon olive oil
- ½ cup chicken stock, low sodium
- 2 tablespoons lime zest, grated
- 2 tablespoons lemon juice
- 1 teaspoon garam masala

Directions:
1. In your slow cooker, mix the trout with the olive oil, lime juice, and the other ingredients, toss, put the lid on and cook on High for 2 hours.
2. Divide everything between plates and serve.

per serving: 200 calories,24.3g protein, 0.6g carbohydrates, 10.6g fat, 0.3g fiber, 67mg cholesterol, 139mg sodium, 433mg potassium.

Tuna and Scallions Mix

Preparation time: 10 minutes
Cooking time: 2 hours
Servings: 4

Ingredients:

- 1-pound tuna fillets, boneless and cubed
- 4 scallions, chopped
- ½ cup coconut cream
- ½ cup chicken stock, low sodium
- 1 tablespoon olive oil
- 1 teaspoon turmeric powder
- A pinch of salt and black pepper
- 1 tablespoon chives, chopped

Directions:

1. In your slow cooker, mix the tuna with the scallions, cream, and the other ingredients, toss, put the lid on and cook on High for 2 hours.
2. Divide the mix into bowls and serve.

per serving: 519 calories,24.9g protein, 3.2g carbohydrates, 46g fat, 1.2g fiber, 0mg cholesterol, 103mg sodium, 138mg potassium.

Salmon and Carrots Bowls

Preparation time: 10 minutes
Cooking time: 3 hours
Servings: 2

Ingredients:

- 1-pound salmon fillets, boneless
- 1 cup baby carrots, peeled
- ½ teaspoon hot paprika
- ½ teaspoon chili powder
- ¼ cup chicken stock, low sodium
- 2 scallions, chopped
- 2 tablespoons chives, chopped

Directions:

1. In your slow cooker, mix the salmon with the carrots, paprika, and the other ingredients, toss, put the lid on and cook on Low for 3 hours.
2. Divide the mix between plates and serve.

per serving: 311 calories,44.6g protein, 2.1g carbohydrates, 14.2g fat, 0.8g fiber, 100mg cholesterol, 208mg sodium, 947mg potassium.

Cod in Sauce

Preparation time: 10 minutes
Cooking time: 3 hours
Servings: 4

Ingredients:

- 1 tablespoon olive oil
- 1-pound cod fillets, boneless
- 2 tablespoons mozzarella, shredded
- ½ cup coconut cream
- ¼ cup chicken stock, low sodium
- 2 garlic cloves, minced
- 1 tablespoon chives, chopped

Directions:

1. In your slow cooker, mix the cod with the oil, mozzarella, and the other ingredients, toss gently, put the lid on, and cook on Low for 3 hours.
2. Divide the mix between plates and serve.

per serving: 233 calories,25.1g protein, 2.7g carbohydrates, 14.2g fat, 0.7g fiber, 48mg cholesterol, 219mg sodium, 88mg potassium.

Vinegar Salmon

Preparation time: 10 minutes
Cooking time: 2 hours
Servings: 4

Ingredients:

- 2 lemons, sliced
- 1-pound wild salmon, skinless and cubed
- ¼ cup balsamic vinegar
- ¼ cup red orange juice
- 1 teaspoon olive oil

Directions:

1. Heat a slow cooker over medium heat, add vinegar, orange juice, and stir well, bring to a simmer for 1 minute and transfer to your Slow cooker.
2. Add salmon, lemon slices, and oil, toss, cover, and cook on High for 2 hours.
3. Divide salmon plates and serve with a side salad.

per serving: 179 calories,22.4g protein, 4.5g carbohydrates, 8.3g fat, 0.8g fiber, 50mg cholesterol, 51mg sodium, 517mg potassium.

Tuna with Handmade Chimichurri

Preparation time: 10 minutes
Cooking time: 1 hour and 15 minutes
Servings: 6

Ingredients:

- ½ cup cilantro, chopped
- 1/3 cup olive oil
- 1 small red onion, chopped
- 3 tablespoons balsamic vinegar
- 2 tablespoons parsley, chopped
- 2 tablespoons basil, chopped
- 1 jalapeno pepper
- 1-pound tuna steak, boneless, skinless, and cubed
- 1 teaspoon red pepper flakes
- 2 garlic cloves, minced
- 1 teaspoon thyme
- 2 avocados, pitted, peeled, and sliced
- 6 ounces baby arugula

Directions:

1. In a bowl, mix the oil with jalapeno, vinegar, onion, cilantro, basil, garlic, parsley, pepper flakes, thyme, whisk well, transfer to your Slow cooker, cover and cook on High for 1 hour. Add tuna, cover, and cook on High for 15 minutes more.
2. Divide arugula on plates, top with tuna slices, drizzle the chimichurri sauce, and serve with avocado slices on the side.

per serving: 390 calories,25g protein, 8.9g carbohydrates, 29.3g fat, 5.5g fiber, 37mg cholesterol, 52mg sodium, 729mg potassium.

Sweet Salmon

Preparation time: 10 minutes
Cooking time: 2 hours
Servings: 4

Ingredients:

- 1-pound salmon fillet
- 1 tablespoon olive oil
- 1 tablespoon stevia

Directions:

1. In a bowl, mix maple extract with mustard and whisk well.
2. Season salmon with salt and pepper, brush with the mustard mix, put in your Slow cooker, cover, and cook on High for 2 hours. Serve the salmon with a side salad.

per serving: 180 calories,22g protein, 0g carbohydrates, 10.5g fat, 0g fiber, 50mg cholesterol, 50mg sodium, 435mg potassium.

Lemon Clams

Preparation time: 10 minutes
Cooking time: 2 hours
Servings: 6

Ingredients:
- 2-pound clams, scrubbed
- 1 tablespoon olive oil
- 3 tablespoons olive oil
- 2 garlic cloves, minced
- Juice of ½ lemon
- 1 small green apple, chopped
- 2 thyme springs, chopped

Directions:
1. Put oil, garlic, salt, pepper, shallot, clams, thyme, lemon juice, and apple in the slow cooker, cover, and cook on High for 2 hours.
2. Divide everything into bowls and serve.

per serving: 171 calories,18.2g protein, 11.1g carbohydrates, 5.8g fat, 0.9g fiber, 42mg cholesterol, 43mg sodium, 528mg potassium.

Parsley Salmon and Relish

Preparation time: 10 minutes
Cooking time: 2 hours
Servings: 4

Ingredients:
- 1-pound salmon fillets, boneless
- 1 shallot, chopped
- 1 tablespoon lemon juice
- 2 tablespoons olive oil
- 2 tablespoons parsley, finely chopped

Directions:
1. Brush salmon fillets with the olive oil, put in your Slow cooker, add the shallot and lemon juice, cover, and cook on High for 2 hours.
2. Shed salmon and divide into 2 bowls.
3. Add oil and parsley and whisk well.
4. Divide this mix over salmon, toss and serve.

per serving: 213 calories,22.2g protein, 0.6g carbohydrates, 14.1g fat, 0.1g fiber, 50mg cholesterol, 52mg sodium, 459mg potassium.

Mussels Chowder

Preparation time: 10 minutes
Cooking time: 2 hours
Servings: 6

Ingredients:
- 2-pound mussels
- 2 cups tomatoes, chopped
- 2 cup of water
- 1 teaspoon red pepper flakes, crushed
- 3 garlic cloves, minced
- 1 handful parsley, chopped
- 1 yellow onion, chopped
- 1 tablespoon olive oil

Directions:
1. In your Slow cooker, mix mussels with tomatoes, water, pepper flakes, garlic, parsley, onion, and oil, stir, cover, and cook on High for 2 hours.
2. Divide into bowls and serve.

per serving: 174 calories,19g protein, 10.6g carbohydrates, 5.8g fat, 1.2g fiber, 42mg cholesterol, 44mg sodium, 523mg potassium.

Fish Mix

Preparation time: 10 minutes
Cooking time: 2 hours
Servings: 4

Ingredients:
- 4 cod fillets
- 1-pound cherry tomatoes halved
- 1 garlic clove, minced
- ¼ cup of water

Directions:
1. Put the stock in your Slow cooker, add fish, tomatoes, thyme, garlic, oil, cover and cook on High for 2 hours.
2. Divide everything between plates and serve.

per serving: 114 calories,21.7g protein, 5.3g carbohydrates, 1.3g fat, 1.7g fiber, 55mg cholesterol, 81mg sodium, 3mg potassium.

Indian Cod

Preparation time: 10 minutes
Cooking time: 2 hours
Servings: 6

Ingredients:

- 6 cod fillets, cut into medium pieces
- 1 tomato, chopped
- 14 ounces of coconut milk
- 2 yellow onions, sliced
- 2 red bell peppers, cut into strips
- 2 garlic cloves, minced
- 6 curry leaves
- 1 tablespoon coriander
- 1 tablespoon ginger, finely grated
- ½ teaspoon turmeric, ground
- 2 teaspoons cumin, ground
- ½ teaspoon fenugreek, ground
- 1 teaspoon hot pepper flakes
- 2 tablespoons lemon juice

Directions:

1. In your Slow cooker, mix fish with tomato, milk, onions, bell peppers, garlic cloves, curry leaves, coriander, turmeric, cumin, fenugreek, pepper flakes, and lemon juice, cover and cook on High for 2 hours.
2. Toss fish, divide the whole mix between plates, and serve.

per serving: 281 calories, 22.7g protein, 12g carbohydrates, 17.2g fat, 3.2g fiber, 55mg cholesterol, 91mg sodium, 368mg potassium.

Cod with Paprika

Preparation time: 15 minutes
Cooking time: 2 hours
Servings: 4

Ingredients:

- 4 cod fillets
- 1 tablespoon parsley, chopped
- 10 ounces peas
- ½ teaspoon oregano, dried
- ½ teaspoon paprika
- 2 garlic cloves, chopped

Directions:

1. In your food processor mix garlic with parsley, oregano, paprika and blend well and add to your Slow cooker.
2. Add fish, peas, salt, and pepper, cover, and cook on High for 2 hours.
3. Divide into bowls and serve.

per serving: 151 calories, 24g protein, 11.1g carbohydrates, 1.4g fat, 3.9g fiber, 55mg cholesterol, 74mg sodium, 193mg potassium.

Nutritious Salmon Bowls

Preparation time: 5 minutes
Cooking time: 2 hours
Servings: 4

Ingredients:
- 4 salmon fillets
- ½ cup of brown rice
- 1 ½ cup water
- 1 tablespoon olive oil

Directions:
1. In your Slow cooker mix stock with rice, water, oil, and stir.
2. Add the salmon, cover, and cook on High for 2 hours.
3. Divide salmon on plates, add rice mix on the side, and serve.

per serving: 351 calories,36.3g protein, 18.1g carbohydrates, 15.1g fat, 0.8g fiber, 78mg cholesterol, 82mg sodium, 748mg potassium.

Sweet Potato and Fish

Preparation time: 10 minutes
Cooking time: 2 hours
Servings: 6

Ingredients:
- 6 cod fillets
- 1 yellow onion, chopped
- 1 cup sweet potato
- 2 cups of water

Directions:
1. In your Slow cooker, mix fish with onion, sweet potatoes, water, cover, and cook on High for 2 hours.
2. Divide into bowls and serve.

per serving: 127 calories,20.9g protein, 8.6g carbohydrates, 1.1g fat, 1.5g fiber, 55mg cholesterol, 85mg sodium, 186mg potassium.

Salmon and Vinaigrette

Preparation time: 2 hours
Cooking time: 2 hours
Servings: 12

Ingredients:
- 6 salmon steaks, cut into halves
- 2 tablespoons olive oil
- 4 leeks, sliced
- 2 garlic cloves, minced
- 2 tablespoons parsley, chopped
- 1 cup clam juice
- 2 tablespoons lemon juice
- 1/3 cup dill, chopped
- 2 tablespoon red raspberries
- 1 tablespoon cider vinegar

Directions:
1. In a bowl, mix red raspberries with vinegar and salmon, toss, cover, and keep in the fridge for 2 hours.
2. In your Slow cooker, mix oil with parsley, leeks, garlic, clam juice, lemon juice, dill, and salmon, cover, and cook on High for 2 hours.
3. Divide everything between plates and serve.

per serving: 171 calories,18.2g protein, 7.6g carbohydrates, 8g fat, 0.9g fiber, 39mg cholesterol, 122mg sodium, 469mg potassium.

Fish and Parsley Pudding

Preparation time: 10 minutes
Cooking time: 2 hours
Servings: 6

Ingredients:
- 1-pound cod fillets, cut into medium pieces
- 2 tablespoons parsley, chopped
- 2 teaspoons lemon juice
- 2 eggs, beaten
- 1 tablespoon olive oil
- ¼ cup of coconut milk

Directions:
1. In a bowl, mix fish with lemon juice, parsley, and stir.
2. Add olive oil to your Slow cooker, add coconut milk and whisk well.
3. Add egg and fish mix, stir, cover and cook on High for 2 hours.
4. Divide between plates and serve with shrimp sauce on top.

per serving: 155 calories,22.1g protein, 0.8g carbohydrates, 7.2g fat, 0.3g fiber, 110mg cholesterol, 93mg sodium, 55mg potassium.

Easy Jambalaya

Preparation time: 10 minutes
Cooking time: 4 hours and 30 minutes
Servings: 12

Ingredients:

- 1 pound chicken breast, chopped
- 1 pound shrimp, peeled and deveined
- 2 tablespoons extra virgin olive oil
- 2 cups onions, chopped
- 1 ½ cup brown rice
- 2 tablespoons garlic, chopped
- 2 cups green, yellow and red bell peppers, chopped
- 3.5 cups water
- 1 cup tomatoes, crushed

Directions:

1. Add the oil to your Slow cooker and spread.
2. Add chicken, onion, rice, garlic, mixed bell peppers, water, tomatoes, and cover and cook on High for 4 hours.
3. Add shrimp, cover, cook on High for 30 minutes more, divide everything between plates and serve.

per serving: 209 calories,19g protein, 22.1g carbohydrates, 4.g fat, 1.7g fiber, 104mg cholesterol, 120mg sodium, 365mg potassium.

Vegetables Tuna Mix

Preparation time: 5 minutes
Cooking time: 2 hours
Servings: 6

Ingredients:

- 6 tuna fillets
- 1 cup mushrooms
- 1 cup peas, frozen
- 3 cups of water
- 4 ounces mozzarella, shredded

Directions:

1. Add water to your Slow cooker, also add tuna, peas, and mushrooms, stir, cover and cook on High for 1 hour.
2. Add cheese all over, cover, cook on High for 1 more hour, divide into bowls and serve.

per serving: 438 calories,28g protein, 4.5g carbohydrates, 34.5g fat, 1.4g fiber, 10mg cholesterol, 119mg sodium, 97mg potassium.

Ginger Mackerel

Preparation time: 10 minutes
Cooking time: 2 hours
Servings: 4

Ingredients:

- 4 mackerel fillets, cut into pieces
- 3 garlic cloves, minced
- 8 shallots, chopped
- 1 teaspoon turmeric powder
- 1 tablespoon chili paste
- 1 small piece of ginger, chopped
- 3 ½ cups water
- 5 tablespoons olive oil

Directions:

1. In your blender, mix garlic with shallots, chili paste, turmeric powder and blend well.
2. Add the oil to your Slow cooker, also add fish, spices paste, ginger, water, and stir, cover, cook on High for 2 hours, divide between plates and serve.

per serving: 413 calories,21.9g protein, 6g carbohydrates, 33.9g fat, 0.2g fiber, 67mg cholesterol, 127mg sodium, 445mg potassium.

Celery and Mackerel

Preparation time: 10 minutes
Cooking time: 2 hours
Servings: 4

Ingredients:

- 4 mackerel, cut into medium pieces
- 1 cup of water
- 1 garlic clove, crushed
- 1 shallot, sliced
- The 1-inch ginger piece, chopped
- 1 sweet onion, thinly sliced
- 2 celery stalks, sliced

Directions:

1. In your Slow cooker, mix, ginger, garlic, and shallot.
2. Add water and mackerel, stir, cover the slow cooker and cook on High for 2 hours.
3. Put onion and celery in a bowl and cover with ice water.
4. Divide mackerel on plates, drain onion and celery well, divide next to mackerel and serve.

per serving: 246 calories,21.5g protein, 3.5g carbohydrates, 15.7g fat, 0.8g fiber, 66mg cholesterol, 83mg sodium, 427mg potassium.

Tender Mackerel

Preparation time: 10 minutes
Cooking time: 2 hours
Servings: 4

Ingredients:
- 4 mackerels
- Juice and rind of 1 lemon
- 1 tablespoon chives, finely chopped
- 1 egg, beaten
- 1 tablespoon olive oil
- 3 lemon wedges

Directions:
1. In a bowl, mix lemon juice, lemon rind, egg, and chives, stir very well, and coat mackerel with this mix.
2. Add the oil to your Slow cooker and arrange mackerel inside.
3. Cover, cook on High for 2 hours, divide fish between plates and serve with lemon wedges on the side.

per serving: 282 calories,22.6g protein, 2g carbohydrates, 20.3g fat, 0.6g fiber,107mg cholesterol, 89mg sodium, 397mg potassium.

Mussels Mix

Preparation time: 5 minutes
Cooking time: 2 hours
Servings: 10

Ingredients:
- 2-pound mussels, scrubbed
- 1 tablespoon olive oil
- 1 yellow onion, chopped
- 1 cup of water
- 1 tablespoon paprika

Directions:
1. Grease your Slow cooker with the oil, add onion, paprika, mussels, and water, cover, and cook on High for 2 hours.
2. Discard unopened mussels, divide the rest between bowls and serve.

per serving: 96 calories,11g protein, 4.8g carbohydrates, 3.5g fat, 0.5g fiber, 25mg cholesterol, 261mg sodium, 323mg potassium.

Seafood Mix

Preparation time: 10 minutes
Cooking time: 2 hours
Servings: 8

Ingredients:
- 15 small clams
- 30 mussels, scrubbed
- 1 cup sweet potatoes, chopped
- 1 yellow onion, chopped
- 1 cup of water
- 2 tablespoons parsley, chopped
- 1 teaspoon olive oil

Directions:
1. Grease your Slow cooker with the oil, add clams, mussels, potatoes, onion, water, and parsley, cover and cook on High for 2 hours.
2. Add parsley, stir, divide into bowls and serve with lemon wedges on the side.

per serving: 98 calories, 9.4g protein, 9.3g carbohydrates, 2.3g fat, 1.1g fiber, 21mg cholesterol, 218mg sodium, 419mg potassium.

Fast Crab Legs

Preparation time: 5 minutes
Cooking time: 1 hour and 30 minutes
Servings: 4

Ingredients:
- 1-pound king crab legs, broken in half
- 3 lemon wedges
- 2 tablespoons olive oil
- ½ cup of water

Directions:
1. In your Slow cooker, mix water with crab legs and olive oil, cover, and cook on High for 1 hour and 30 minutes.
2. Divide crab legs between bowls and serve with lemon wedges on the side.

per serving: 168 calories, 21.4g protein, 0.5g carbohydrates, 9g fat, 0.2g fiber, 60mg cholesterol, 125mg sodium, 8mg potassium.

Easy Shrimp Boil

Preparation time: 10 minutes
Cooking time: 2 hours and 30 minutes
Servings: 4

Ingredients:
- 1 pounds shrimp, head removed
- 1 cup of water
- 1 teaspoon red pepper flakes, crushed
- 2 sweet onions, cut into wedges
- 8 garlic cloves, crushed

Directions:
1. In your Slow cooker mix water with red pepper flakes, onions, garlic, and cover and cook on High for 2 hours.
2. Add shrimp, cover, cook on High for 30 minutes more, divide into bowls.

per serving: 167 calories,26.9g protein, 9.1g carbohydrates, 2.1g fat, 1.4g fiber, 239mg cholesterol, 182mg sodium, 306mg potassium.

Shrimp Curry

Preparation time: 10 minutes
Cooking time: 2 hours
Servings: 4

Ingredients:
- 1 pound shrimp, peeled and deveined
- 1 cup of water
- 4 lemon slices
- ½ teaspoon curry powder
- ¼ cup mushrooms, sliced
- ¼ cup yellow onion, chopped
- 1 tablespoon olive oil

Directions:
1. In your Slow cooker, mix water with lemon, curry powder, mushrooms, onion, whisk well, cover, and cook on High for 2 hours.
2. Divide curry into bowls and serve.

per serving: 171 calories,26.2g protein, 3.3g carbohydrates, 5.5g fat, 0.5g fiber, 239mg cholesterol, 179mg sodium, 231mg potassium.

Shrimp Mix

Preparation time: 10 minutes
Cooking time: 1 hour
Servings: 4

Ingredients:
- 1-pound shrimp, peeled and deveined
- 2 tablespoons olive oil
- 1 tablespoon yellow onion, chopped
- 1 cup of water
- 1 tablespoon dill, chopped

Directions:
1. In your Slow cooker, mix oil with onion, dill, and shrimp, cover, and cook on High for 1 hour.
2. Divide everything into bowls and serve.

per serving: 198 calories,26g protein, 2.4g carbohydrates, 9g fat, 0.2g fiber, 239mg cholesterol, 180mg sodium, 26mg potassium.

Pineapple Shrimp

Preparation time: 10 minutes
Cooking time: 1 hour
Servings: 4

Ingredients:
- 1-pound shrimp, peeled and deveined
- ½ pound pea pods
- 3 tablespoons vinegar
- ¾ cup pineapple juice
- 1 cup of water

Directions:
1. Put shrimp and pea pods in your Slow cooker, add vinegar, pineapple juice, stock and stir, cover and cook on High for 1 hour,
2. Divide between plates and serve.

per serving: 186 calories,27.6g protein, 12.1g carbohydrates, 2.1g fat, 1.6g fiber, 239mg cholesterol, 282mg sodium, 375mg potassium.

Oregano Octopus

Preparation time: 1 hour and 10 minutes
Cooking time: 3 hours
Servings: 6

Ingredients:
- 1 octopus, cleaned and prepared
- 2 rosemary springs
- 2 teaspoons oregano, dried
- ½ yellow onion, roughly chopped
- 4 thyme sprigs
- ½ lemon
- 1 teaspoon black peppercorns
- 3 tablespoons extra virgin olive oil
- 4 garlic cloves, minced

Directions:
1. Put the octopus in your Slow cooker, add oregano, 2 rosemary springs, 4 thyme springs, onion, lemon, 3 tablespoons olive oil, peppercorns and stir, cover, and cook on High for 2 hours.
2. Transfer octopus on a cutting board, cut tentacles, put them in a bowl, mix with remaining ingredients, toss to coat, and leave aside for 1 hour.
3. Transfer octopus and the marinade to your Slow cooker again, cover, and cook on High for 1 more hour.
4. Divide octopus on plates, drizzle the marinade all over, and serve.

per serving: 94 calories,4.6g protein, 3.2g carbohydrates, 7.4g fat, 0.7g fiber, 13mg cholesterol, 66mg sodium, 41mg potassium.

Nutritious Squid

Preparation time: 10 minutes
Cooking time: 3 hours
Servings: 4

Ingredients:
- 4 squid
- 1 cup brown rice, cooked
- 1 teaspoon minced garlic
- 1 cup of water

Directions:
1. Fill the squid with brown rice and minced garlic and put it in the slow cooker.
2. Add water and cook the squid on high for 3 hours.

per serving: 196 calories,7.8g protein, 36.7g carbohydrates, 1.6g fat, 1.6g fiber, 0mg cholesterol, 4mg sodium, 131mg potassium.

Aromatic Squid

Preparation time: 10 minutes
Cooking time: 3 hours
Servings: 4

Ingredients:

- 17 ounces squids
- 1 ½ tablespoon red chili powder
- ¼ teaspoon turmeric powder
- 2 cups of water
- 4 garlic cloves, minced
- ½ teaspoons cumin seeds
- 3 tablespoons olive oil
- ¼ teaspoon mustard seeds
- 1-inch ginger pieces, chopped

Directions:

1. Put squids in your Slow cooker, add chili powder, turmeric, and water, stir, cover, and cook on High for 2 hours.
2. In your blender, mix ginger, oil, garlic, and cumin and blend well.
3. Add this over the squids, cover, and cook on High for 1 more hour.
4. Divide everything into bowls and serve.

per serving: 217 calories,19.4g protein, 6.5g carbohydrates, 12.8g fat, 1.1g fiber, 281mg cholesterol, 86mg sodium, 373mg potassium.

Shrimp with Vegetables

Preparation time: 5 minutes
Cooking time: 1 hour
Servings: 6

Ingredients:

- 1-pound shrimp, peeled and deveined
- 2 teaspoons avocado oil
- 1 eggplant, cubed
- 2 tomatoes, cubed
- Juice of 1 lime
- ½ cup of water
- 4 garlic cloves, minced
- 1 tablespoon coriander, chopped
- 1 tablespoon chives, chopped

Directions:

1. In your slow cooker, mix the shrimp with the oil, eggplant, tomatoes, and the other ingredients, toss, put the lid on and cook on High for 1 hour.
2. Divide the mix into bowls and serve.

per serving: 125 calories,18.6g protein, 9.2g carbohydrates, 1.7g fat, 3.6g fiber, 159mg cholesterol, 189mg sodium, 427mg potassium.

Sea Bass with Spices

Preparation time: 10 minutes
Cooking time: 3 hours
Servings: 6

Ingredients:

- 1-pound sea bass, boneless and cubed
- 1 cup butternut squash, peeled and cubed
- 1 teaspoon olive oil
- ½ teaspoon turmeric powder
- ½ teaspoon Italian seasoning
- 1 cup of water
- 1 tablespoon cilantro, chopped

Directions:

1. In your slow cooker, mix the sea bass with the squash, oil, turmeric, and the other ingredients, toss, the lid on, and cook on Low for 3 hours.
2. Divide everything between plates and serve.

per serving: 140 calories,14.9g protein, 2.9g carbohydrates, 7.9g fat, 0.5g fiber, 0mg cholesterol, 2mg sodium, 88mg potassium.

Oregano and Parsley Clams

Preparation time: 10 minutes
Cooking time: 2 hours
Servings: 12

Ingredients:

- 2 tablespoons olive oil
- 36 clams, scrubbed
- 1 teaspoon red pepper flakes, crushed
- 1 teaspoon parsley, chopped
- 5 garlic cloves, minced
- 1 tablespoon oregano, dried
- 2 cups of water

Directions:

1. In your Slow cooker, mix olive oil with clams, pepper flakes, parsley, garlic, oregano, and water, stir, cover, and cook on High for 2 hours.
2. Divide into bowls and serve.

per serving: 65 calories,5.9g protein, 2.5g carbohydrates, 3.5g fat, 0.2g fiber, 13mg cholesterol, 139mg sodium, 169mg potassium.

Clam Soup

Preparation time: 10 minutes
Cooking time: 2 hours
Servings: 6

Ingredients:

- 1 cup celery stalks, chopped
- 1 teaspoon thyme, ground
- 2 cups of water
- 14 ounces baby clams
- 2 cups organic almond milk
- 1 cup onion, chopped

Directions:

1. Heat the pan over medium heat, add celery and onion, stir and cook for 5 minutes.
2. Transfer everything to your Slow cooker, add baby clams, water, thyme, and almond milk, stir and cook on High for 2 hours.
3. Divide into bowls and serve.

per serving: 227 calories, 2.6g protein, 14.1g carbohydrates, 19.3g fat, 2.8g fiber, 0mg cholesterol, 268mg sodium, 343mg potassium.

Shrimp and Mint Bowls

Preparation time: 10 minutes
Cooking time: 1 hour
Servings: 6

Ingredients:

- 2 tablespoons olive oil
- 1-pound shrimp, peeled and deveined
- 2 tablespoons lime juice
- 3 endives, leaves separated
- 3 tablespoons parsley, chopped
- 2 teaspoons mint, chopped
- 1 tablespoon tarragon, chopped
- 1 tablespoon lemon juice
- 1 teaspoon lime zest

Directions:

1. In a bowl, mix shrimp olive oil, toss to coat, and spread into the Slow cooker,
2. Add lime juice, endives, parsley, mint, tarragon, lemon juice, lemon zest, toss, cover, and cook on High for 1 hour.
3. Divide into bowls and serve.

per serving: 176 calories, 20.6g protein, 10.2g carbohydrates, 6.5g fat, 8.1g fiber, 159mg cholesterol, 243mg sodium, 961mg potassium.

Creole Shrimp

Preparation time: 10 minutes
Cooking time: 1 hour and 30 minutes
Servings: 5

Ingredients:
- ½ pound big shrimp, peeled and deveined
- 2 teaspoons olive oil
- Juice of 1 lemon
- 1 teaspoon Creole seasoning

Directions:
1. In your Slow cooker, mix shrimp with oil, lemon juice, and Creole seasoning, toss, cover, and cook on High for 1 hour and 30 minutes.
2. Divide into bowls and serve.

per serving: 78 calories,11.9g protein, 0.5g carbohydrates, 3g fat, 0.2g fiber, 111mg cholesterol, 97mg sodium, 110mg potassium.

Octopus Mix

Preparation time: 1 day
Cooking time: 3 hours
Servings: 4

Ingredients:
- 1 octopus, already prepared
- 1 cup of water
- 1 cup olive oil
- 2 teaspoons pepper sauce
- 1 tablespoon paprika
- ½ bunch parsley, chopped
- 2 garlic cloves, minced
- 1 yellow onion, chopped

Directions:
1. Put the octopus in a bowl, add water, half of the oil, pepper sauce, paprika, and parsley, toss to coat, cover, and keep in a cold place for 1 day.
2. Add the rest of the oil to your Slow cooker and arrange onions on the bottom.
3. Add the octopus and the marinade, stir, cover, cook on High for 3 hours, divide everything between plates and serve.

per serving: 456 calories,1.9g protein, 4g carbohydrates, 50.7g fat, 1.3g fiber, 0mg cholesterol, 4mg sodium, 87mg potassium.

Poultry

Rosemary Chicken Mix

Preparation time: 10 minutes
Cooking time: 6 hours
Servings: 4

Ingredients:
- 1 tablespoon olive oil
- 1-pound chicken breast, skinless, boneless, and roughly cubed
- ¾ cup chicken stock, low sodium
- 1 teaspoon ground paprika
- 1 teaspoon rosemary, dried
- 1 tablespoon lemon juice
- 1 tablespoon chives, chopped

Directions:
1. In your slow cooker, mix the chicken with the oil, and the other ingredients, toss, put the lid on, and cook on Low for 6 hours.
2. Divide the mix into bowls and serve.

per serving: 191 calories,25.7g protein, 2.7g carbohydrates, 8.2g fat, 1.2g fiber, 73mg cholesterol, 202mg sodium, 483mg potassium.

Citrus Chicken Mix

Preparation time: 10 minutes
Cooking time: 7 hours
Servings: 4

Ingredients:
- 1-pound chicken thighs, boneless and skinless
- 1 tablespoon olive oil
- Juice of 1 lime
- Zest of 1 lime, grated
- ½ cup tomato sauce, low sodium
- 2 spring onions, chopped
- 1 tablespoon oregano, chopped

Directions:
1. In your slow cooker, mix the chicken with the oil, lime juice, and the other ingredients, toss, put the lid on and cook on Low for 7 hours.
2. Divide the mix between plates and serve.

per serving: 264 calories,33.7g protein, 4.7g carbohydrates, 12.1g fat, 1.6g fiber, 101mg cholesterol, 259mg sodium, 435mg potassium.

Chicken with Peppercorns

Preparation time: 10 minutes
Cooking time: 7 hours
Servings: 4

Ingredients:

- 1 pound chicken breasts, skinless, boneless
- 2 red onions, sliced
- ½ cup chicken stock, low sodium
- ½ cup tomato passata, low sodium
- 2 teaspoons olive oil
- 1 teaspoon black peppercorns, crushed
- 2 garlic cloves, minced
- 1 tablespoon chives, chopped

Directions:

1. Grease the slow cooker with the oil and mix the chicken with the onions, stock, and the other ingredients inside.
2. Put the lid on, cook on Low for 7 hours, divide between plates, and serve.

per serving: 266 calories,33.9g protein, 6.9g carbohydrates, 10.9g fat, 1.4g fiber, 101mg cholesterol, 196mg sodium, 373mg potassium.

Greens Chicken Mix

Preparation time: 10 minutes
Cooking time: 6 hours and 10 minutes
Servings: 4

Ingredients:

- 1-pound chicken breast, skinless, boneless and cut into strips
- 1 tablespoon basil pesto, low sodium
- 1 tablespoon olive oil
- 4 scallions, chopped
- 1 cup chicken stock, low sodium
- 1 tablespoon cilantro, chopped

Directions:

1. Heat a pan with the oil over medium-high heat, add the scallions and the meat, brown for 10 minutes, transfer to the slow cooker and mix with the remaining ingredients.
2. Toss, put the lid on, cook on Low for 6 hours, divide the mix between plates and serve.

per serving: 170 calories,24.5g protein, 1.4g carbohydrates, 6.8g fat, 0.4g fiber, 73mg cholesterol, 269mg sodium, 468mg potassium.

Chives Chicken

Preparation time: 10 minutes
Cooking time: 7 hours
Servings: 4

Ingredients:

- 1-pound chicken thighs, boneless, skinless, and sliced
- 1 tablespoon avocado oil
- 1 teaspoon cumin, ground
- 1 tablespoon rosemary, chopped
- 1 cup chicken stock, low sodium
- 1 tablespoon chives, chopped

Directions:

1. In your slow cooker, mix the chicken with the oil, cumin, and the other ingredients, toss, put the lid on and cook on Low for 7 hours.
2. Divide the mix between plates and serve.

per serving: 228 calories,33.2g protein, 1.2g carbohydrates, 9.2g fat, 0.6g fiber, 101mg cholesterol, 290mg sodium, 310mg potassium.

Chicken and Eggplant Mix

Preparation time: 10 minutes
Cooking time: 5 hours and 10 minutes.
Servings: 4

Ingredients:

- 1 pound chicken breast, skinless, boneless
- 1 red onion, sliced
- 1 tablespoon olive oil
- ½ teaspoon cumin, ground
- ½ teaspoon sweet paprika
- 1 cup chicken stock, low sodium
- 1 teaspoon coriander, ground
- ½ cup canned tomatoes, crushed, low sodium
- ½ teaspoon red pepper flakes, crushed
- 1 small eggplant, cubed
- 1 tablespoon oregano, chopped

Directions:

1. Heat a pan with the oil over medium-high heat, add the chicken, onion, and pepper flakes, stir, brown for 10 minutes, and transfer to your slow cooker. Add the rest of the ingredients, toss, put the lid on, and cook on High for 5 hours.
2. Divide everything between plates and serve.

per serving: 251 calories,27.6g protein, 20.9g carbohydrates, 7.3g fat, 11.2g fiber, 73mg cholesterol, 257mg sodium, 1179mg potassium.

Chicken Saute

Preparation time: 10 minutes
Cooking time: 7 hours
Servings: 4

Ingredients:

- 1-pound chicken breast, skinless, boneless, and cubed
- 1 tablespoon yellow curry paste
- 1 yellow onion, chopped
- 1 tablespoon olive oil
- 1 teaspoon basil, dried
- 1 teaspoon black peppercorns, crushed
- 1 cup chicken stock
- ¼ cup coconut cream
- 1 tablespoon lime juice
- 1 tablespoon cilantro, chopped

Directions:

1. In your slow cooker, mix the chicken with the curry paste, onion, and the other ingredients, toss, put the lid on and cook on Low for 7 hours.
2. Divide everything into bowls and serve hot.

per serving: 231 calories,24.9g protein, 4.7g carbohydrates, 12.4g fat, 1.8g fiber, 73mg cholesterol, 354mg sodium, 711mg potassium.

Lemon Juice Chicken Mix

Preparation time: 10 minutes
Cooking time: 5 hours
Servings: 4

Ingredients:

- 1-pound chicken breast, skinless, boneless, and sliced
- ½ cup parsley, chopped
- 2 tablespoons olive oil
- 1 tablespoon pine nuts
- 1 tablespoon lemon juice
- ½ cup chicken stock, low sodium
- 1 teaspoon hot paprika

Directions:

1. In a blender, mix the parsley with the oil, pine nuts, and lemon juice and pulse well.
2. In your slow cooker, mix the chicken with the parsley mix and the remaining ingredients, toss, put the lid on and cook on High for 5 hours. Divide everything between plates and serve.

per serving: 218 calories,24.7g protein, 1.5g carbohydrates, 12.4g fat, 0.6g fiber, 73mg cholesterol, 232mg sodium, 481mg potassium.

Pearl Onions Turkey

Preparation time: 10 minutes
Cooking time: 6 hours
Servings: 2

Ingredients:

- 1 pound turkey breasts, skinless, boneless, and roughly cubed
- 1 tablespoon olive oil
- ½ cup pearl onions, peeled
- 1 cup chicken stock, low sodium
- 1 tablespoon Italian seasoning

Directions:

1. In your slow cooker, mix the turkey with onions and the other ingredients, toss, put the lid on and cook on Low for 6 hours.
2. Divide the mix between plates and serve.

per serving: 233 calories, 25.1g protein, 2.7g carbohydrates, 14.2g fat, 0.7g fiber, 48mg cholesterol, 219mg sodium, 88mg potassium.

Turkey and Mushrooms

Preparation time: 10 minutes
Cooking time: 6 hours
Servings: 5

Ingredients:

- 1 pound turkey, skinless, boneless, and sliced
- 1 cup chicken stock, low sodium
- 1 cup white mushrooms, sliced
- ½ teaspoon rosemary, dried
- ½ teaspoon cumin, ground
- ½ cup coconut cream
- 1 tablespoon olive oil
- ¼ cup chives, chopped

Directions:

1. In your slow cooker, mix the turkey with the stock, mushrooms, and the other ingredients, toss, put the lid on, and cook on Low for 6 hours.
2. Divide everything between plates and serve.

per serving: 240 calories, 27.8g protein, 2.2g carbohydrates, 13.3g fat, 0.8g fiber, 69mg cholesterol, 393mg sodium, 88mg potassium.

Turkey with Sauce

Preparation time: 10 minutes
Cooking time: 7 hours
Servings: 4

Ingredients:

- 1 cup tomato sauce, low sodium
- ½ cup chicken stock, low sodium
- ½ tablespoon rosemary, chopped
- 1-pound turkey breast, skinless, boneless, and roughly cubed
- 1 tablespoon cilantro, chopped

Directions:

1. In your slow cooker, mix the turkey with the sauce, stock, and the other ingredients, toss, put the lid on and cook on Low for 7 hours.
2. Divide everything between plates and serve.

per serving: 134 calories,20.2g protein, 8.3g carbohydrates, 2.1g fat, 1.7g fiber, 49mg cholesterol, 147mg sodium, 551mg potassium.

Chicken and Chickpeas

Preparation time: 10 minutes
Cooking time: 7 hours
Servings: 4

Ingredients:

- 1 tablespoon olive oil
- 1 red onion, chopped
- 1 cup chickpeas, boiled
- 1-pound chicken breast, skinless, boneless, and cubed
- ½ cup cherry tomatoes halved
- ½ teaspoon rosemary, dried
- ½ teaspoon turmeric powder
- 1 cup chicken stock, low sodium
- 1 tablespoon chives, chopped

Directions:

1. Grease the slow cooker with the oil and mix the chicken with the onion, chickpeas, and the other ingredients inside the pot.
2. Put the lid on, cook on Low for 7 hours, divide between plates, and serve.

per serving: 362 calories,34.5g protein, 34.6g carbohydrates, 9.6g fat, 9.7g fiber, 73mg cholesterol, 265mg sodium, 912mg potassium.

Turkey with Leeks

Preparation time: 10 minutes
Cooking time: 6 hours
Servings: 4

Ingredients:

- 1 pound turkey breast, skinless, boneless, and cubed
- 1 leek, sliced
- 1 cup radishes, sliced
- 1 red onion, chopped
- 1 tablespoon olive oil
- 1 cup chicken stock, low sodium
- ½ teaspoon coriander, ground
- 1 tablespoon cilantro, chopped

Directions:

1. In your slow cooker, combine the turkey with the leek, radishes, onion, and the other ingredients, toss, put the lid on and cook on High for 6 hours. Divide everything between plates and serve.

per serving: 173 calories,17.8g protein, 12.6g carbohydrates, 5.7g fat, 1.5g fiber, 39mg cholesterol, 138mg sodium, 636mg potassium.

Parsley and Onions Turkey

Preparation time: 10 minutes
Cooking time: 5 hours
Servings: 4

Ingredients:

- 1 yellow onion, chopped
- 1 tablespoon olive oil
- 1 cup coconut cream
- ½ teaspoon curry powder
- 1-pound turkey breast, skinless, boneless, and cubed
- 1 teaspoon turmeric powder
- ½ cup of water
- 1 tablespoon parsley, chopped

Directions:

1. In your slow cooker, mix the turkey with the onion, oil, and the other ingredients except for the cream and the parsley, stir, put the lid on and cook on High for 4 hours and 30 minutes.
2. Add the remaining ingredients, toss, put the lid on again, cook on High for 30 minutes more, divide the mix between plates, and serve.

per serving: 300 calories,21.1g protein, 11.2g carbohydrates, 19.8g fat, 2.7g fiber, 49mg cholesterol, 116mg sodium, 564mg potassium.

Hot Chicken

Preparation time: 10 minutes
Cooking time: 6 hours
Servings: 4

Ingredients:

- 1-pound chicken breasts, skinless, boneless, and cubed
- 1 zucchini, cubed
- 2 garlic cloves, minced
- 1 red chili, minced
- ½ teaspoon hot paprika
- 1 red onion, chopped
- 2 tablespoons olive oil
- 1 cup of water
- 1 tablespoon chives, chopped

Directions:

1. In your slow cooker, mix the chicken with the zucchini, garlic, chili pepper, and the other ingredients, toss, put the lid on and cook on Low for 6 hours.
2. Divide everything between plates and serve.

per serving: 297 calories,33.8g protein, 4.8g carbohydrates, 15.6g fat, 1.2g fiber, 101mg cholesterol, 106mg sodium, 4.5mg potassium.

Turkey with Spices and Vegetables

Preparation time: 10 minutes
Cooking time: 7 hours
Servings: 4

Ingredients:

- 1 tablespoon olive oil
- 2 scallions, minced
- 1-pound turkey breast, skinless, boneless, and cubed
- 2 garlic cloves, minced
- 1 cup radishes, sliced
- ½ cup of water
- ½ teaspoon coriander, ground
- 1 tablespoon parsley, chopped

Directions:

1. In your slow cooker, mix the turkey with the oil, scallions, and the other ingredients, toss, put the lid on and cook on Low for 7 hours.
2. Divide the mix between plates and serve.

per serving: 158 calories,19.8g protein, 6.9g carbohydrates, 5.4g fat, 1.3g fiber, 49mg cholesterol, 116mg sodium, 643mg potassium.

Chives Chicken

Preparation time: 10 minutes
Cooking time: 20 minutes
Servings: 4

Ingredients:
- 1-pound chicken breasts, boneless, skinless, and sliced
- 1 tablespoon olive oil
- 1 red bell pepper, cut into strips
- 1 yellow onion, chopped
- 1 cup of water
- ½ cup coconut cream
- 1 tablespoon chives, chopped

Directions:
1. Set the instant pot on Sauté mode, add the oil, heat it, add the onion and the bell pepper and sauté for 5 minutes.
2. Add the chicken and the rest of the ingredients except the chives put the lid on, and cook on High for 15 minutes.
3. Release the pressure naturally for 10 minutes, divide everything between plates, sprinkle the chives on top, and serve.

per serving: 335 calories,34.1g protein, 6.5g carbohydrates, 19.2g fat, 1.7g fiber, 101mg cholesterol, 106mg sodium, 453mg potassium.

Cilantro Chicken

Preparation time: 10 minutes
Cooking time: 7 hours
Servings: 4

Ingredients:
- 1-pound chicken breasts, skinless, boneless, and sliced
- 2 eggplants, roughly cubed
- 1 cup of water
- 3 scallions, chopped
- 1 teaspoon chili powder
- 1 tablespoon cilantro, chopped

Directions:
1. In your slow cooker, mix the chicken with the eggplant, water, and the other ingredients, toss, put the lid on, cook on Low for 7 hours, divide the mix between plates and serve.

per serving: 290 calories,35.8g protein, 17.3g carbohydrates, 9g fat, 10.2g fiber, 101mg cholesterol, 113mg sodium, 948mg potassium.

Garam Masala Chicken with Vegetables

Preparation time: 10 minutes
Cooking time: 7 hours
Servings: 4

Ingredients:

- 1-pound chicken breasts, skinless, boneless, and roughly cubed
- 1 tablespoon olive oil
- 1 cup Brussels sprouts, halved
- ½ teaspoon garam masala
- 1 cup of water
- 1 tablespoon olive oil
- 1 red onion, sliced
- 1 tablespoon cilantro, chopped

Directions:

1. In your slow cooker, mix the chicken with the sprouts, oil, and the other ingredients, toss, put the lid on and cook on Low for 7 hours.
2. Divide the mix between plates and serve right away.

per serving: 266 calories,36.9g protein, 4.6g carbohydrates, 12g fat, 1.4g fiber, 101mg cholesterol, 107mg sodium, 403mg potassium.

Sweet Mango Chicken

Preparation time: 10 minutes
Cooking time: 5 hours
Servings: 4

Ingredients:

- 1-pound chicken breast, skinless, boneless, and sliced
- 1 cup mango, peeled and cubed
- 4 scallions, chopped
- 1 tablespoon avocado oil
- ½ teaspoon chili powder
- ½ teaspoon rosemary, dried
- 1 cup of water
- 1 tablespoon chives, chopped

Directions:

1. In your slow cooker, mix the chicken with the mango, scallions, chili powder, and the other ingredients, toss, put the lid on and cook on Low for 5 hours.
2. Divide the mix between plates and serve.

per serving: 165 calories,24.8g protein, 7.8g carbohydrates, 3.6g fat, 1.4g fiber, 73mg cholesterol, 66mg sodium, 552mg potassium.

Avocado Turkey

Preparation time: 10 minutes
Cooking time: 6 hours
Servings: 4

Ingredients:

- 1 pound turkey breasts, skinless, boneless, and cubed
- 1 cup avocado, peeled, pitted, and cubed
- 1 cup tomatoes, cubed
- 1 tablespoon chives, chopped
- ½ teaspoon chili powder
- 4 garlic cloves, minced
- ¼ cup of water

Directions:

1. In a slow cooker, mix the turkey with the tomatoes, chives, and the other ingredients except for the avocado, toss, put the lid on and cook on Low for 5 hours and 30 minutes.
2. Add the avocado, toss, cook on Low for 30 minutes more, divide everything between plates and serve.

per serving: 206 calories,20.7g protein, 10.9g carbohydrates, 10.2g fat, 3.8g fiber, 49mg cholesterol, 116mg sodium, 647mg potassium.

Peppers and Chicken Bowls

Preparation time: 10 minutes
Cooking time: 6 hours
Servings: 4

Ingredients:

- 1-pound chicken breasts, skinless, boneless, and cubed
- 2 red bell peppers, cut into strips
- 1 teaspoon olive oil
- ½ teaspoon rosemary, dried
- ½ teaspoon coriander, ground
- 1 cup of water

Directions:

1. In your slow cooker, mix the chicken with the peppers, and the other ingredients, toss, put the lid on, and cook on Low for 6 hours.
2. Divide everything between plates and serve.

per serving: 245 calories,33.4g protein, 4.6g carbohydrates, 9.7g fat, 0.9g fiber, 9.7mg cholesterol, 101mg sodium, 390mg potassium.

Cilantro, Cumin, and Chicken Mix

Preparation time: 5 minutes
Cooking time: 7 hours
Servings: 4

Ingredients:

- 1-pound chicken breasts, skinless, boneless, and halved
- 2 cups red cabbage, shredded
- 1 cup of water
- ½ teaspoon rosemary, dried
- 2 teaspoons cumin, ground
- ¼ cup cilantro, chopped

Directions:

1. In a slow cooker, mix the chicken with the cabbage, water, and the other ingredients, toss, put the lid on and cook on Low for 7 hours.
2. Divide everything between plates and serve.

per serving: 229 calories, 33.5g protein, 2.6g carbohydrates, 8.7g fat, 1.1g fiber, 101mg cholesterol, 108mg sodium, 361mg potassium.

Turkey and Chard

Preparation time: 10 minutes
Cooking time: 6 hours
Servings: 4

Ingredients:

- 1-pound turkey breasts, skinless, boneless, and cubed
- 2 teaspoons olive oil
- 1 cup red chard, torn
- 1 cup of water
- 2 tablespoons lime juice
- 1 tablespoon lime zest, grated

Directions:

1. In your slow cooker, mix the turkey with the oil, and the other ingredients, toss, put the lid on, and cook on Low for 6 hours.
2. Divide everything into bowls and serve.

per serving: 141 calories, 19.7g protein, 5.4g carbohydrates, 4.2g fat, 0.9g fiber, 49mg cholesterol, 117mg sodium, 345mg potassium.

Turkey mix

Preparation time: 10 minutes
Cooking time: 6 hours
Servings: 4

Ingredients:

- 1-pound turkey breast, skinless, boneless, and sliced
- ½ teaspoon red pepper flakes, crushed
- ½ teaspoon turmeric powder
- 1 cup bbq sauce, low sodium
- ¼ cup cilantro, chopped
- 1 cup of water

Directions:

1. In a slow cooker, mix the turkey with the pepper flakes and the other ingredients, toss, put the lid on and cook on Low for 6 hours.
2. Divide everything between plates and serve.

per serving: 214 calories,19.4g protein, 27.8g carbohydrates, 2.1g fat, 1.1g fiber, 49mg cholesterol, 185mg sodium, 490mg potassium.

Chicken and Tomatoes

Preparation time: 10 minutes
Cooking time: 5 hours
Servings: 4

Ingredients:

- 1-pound chicken breast, skinless, boneless, and cubed
- 1 cup asparagus, sliced
- 1 tablespoon olive oil
- 2 scallions, chopped
- 1 teaspoon garam masala
- 1 cup of water
- 1 cup tomatoes, cubed
- 1 tablespoon parsley, chopped

Directions:

1. In your slow cooker, mix the chicken with the asparagus, oil, and the other ingredients except for the asparagus, toss, put the lid on and cook on High for 4 hours.
2. Add the asparagus, toss, cook on High for 1 more hour, divide everything between plates and serve.

per serving: 177 calories,25.4g protein, 3.7g carbohydrates, 6.5g fat, 1.5g fiber, 73mg cholesterol, 65mg sodium, 620mg potassium.

Turkey and Sweet Potatoes

Preparation time: 10 minutes
Cooking time: 7 hours
Servings: 4

Ingredients:

- 1-pound turkey breast, skinless, boneless, and cubed
- 2 teaspoons olive oil
- 1 tablespoon lemon juice
- 2 sweet potatoes, peeled and cubed
- 1 red onion, chopped
- ½ cup tomato sauce
- ¼ cup chicken stock
- 1 tablespoon chives, chopped

Directions:

1. In your slow cooker, mix the turkey with the oil, lemon juice, sweet potatoes, and the other ingredients, toss, put the lid on and cook on Low for 7 hours.
2. Divide everything between plates and serve.

per serving: 202 calories, 20.7g protein, 19.6g carbohydrates, 4.4g fat, 3.2g fiber, 49mg cholesterol, 136mg sodium, 798mg potassium.

Coriander Chicken with Okra

Preparation time: 10 minutes
Cooking time: 5 hours
Servings: 4

Ingredients:

- 1-pound turkey breasts, skinless, boneless, and cubed
- 1 cup okra, halved
- 1 tablespoon lime zest, grated
- ½ cup of water
- 1 tablespoon lime juice
- 1 teaspoon olive oil
- ½ teaspoon coriander, ground
- ½ teaspoon oregano, dried
- 1 teaspoon chili powder

Directions:

1. In your slow cooker, mix the turkey with the okra, lime zest, juice, and the other ingredients, toss, put the lid on and cook on High for 5 hours.
2. Divide everything between plates and serve.

per serving: 141 calories, 20g protein, 7.4g carbohydrates, 3.2g fat, 1.8g fiber, 49mg cholesterol, 116mg sodium, 436mg potassium.

Chicken Mix

Preparation time: 10 minutes
Cooking time: 5 hours
Servings: 4

Ingredients:
- 2 teaspoons olive oil
- 1 red onion, sliced
- 1-pound chicken fillet, cut into strips
- 1 tablespoon lemon juice
- ¾ cup of water
- 1 tablespoon coriander, chopped

Directions:
1. In your slow cooker, mix the chicken with the oil, onion, and the other ingredients, toss, put the lid on and cook on High for 5 hours.
2. Divide the mix between plates and serve with a side salad.

per serving: 247 calories,33.2g protein, 2.7g carbohydrates, 10.8g fat, 0.6g fiber, 101mg cholesterol, 101mg sodium, 322mg potassium.

Citrus Chicken Bowls

Preparation time: 10 minutes
Cooking time: 6 hours
Servings: 4

Ingredients:
- 1-pound chicken breast, skinless, boneless, and cubed
- 1 cup oranges, peeled and cut into segments
- 2 teaspoons olive oil
- 1 teaspoon turmeric powder
- 1 teaspoon balsamic vinegar
- 4 scallions, minced
- 1 cup of orange juice
- 1 tablespoon mint, chopped

Directions:
1. In your slow cooker, mix the chicken with the oranges, scallions, and the other ingredients, toss, put the lid on and cook on Low for 6 hours.
2. Divide the mix between plates and serve.

per serving: 206 calories,25.2g protein, 13.3g carbohydrates, 5.4g fat, 1.8g fiber, 73mg cholesterol, 61mg sodium, 688mg potassium.

Tender Carrot and Chicken Mix

Preparation time: 10 minutes
Cooking time: 7 hours
Servings: 4

Ingredients:

- 1-pound turkey breasts, skinless, boneless, and cubed
- 1 cup carrots, peeled and sliced
- 2 tablespoons avocado oil
- 1 tablespoon balsamic vinegar
- 2 scallions, chopped
- 1 teaspoon turmeric powder
- 1 cup of water
- ½ cup chives, chopped

Directions:

1. In your slow cooker, mix the turkey with the carrots, oil, vinegar, and the other ingredients, toss, put the lid on and cook on Low for 7 hours.
2. Divide the mix between plates and serve right away.

per serving: 145 calories,20.1g protein, 9.1g carbohydrates, 2.9g fat, 2g fiber, 49mg cholesterol, 117mg sodium, 508mg potassium.

Rosemary Chicken Masala

Preparation time: 10 minutes
Cooking time: 7 hours
Servings: 4

Ingredients:

- 1-pound chicken thighs, boneless
- 1 teaspoon rosemary, dried
- ½ teaspoon garam masala
- 1 tablespoon olive oil
- ½ cup of water
- 1 tablespoon cilantro, chopped

Directions:

1. In your slow cooker, mix the chicken with the rosemary, and the other ingredients, toss, put the lid on, and cook on Low for 7 hours.
2. Divide the chicken between plates and serve with a side salad.

per serving: 247 calories,32.8g protein, 0.2g carbohydrates, 12g fat, 0.1g fiber, 101mg cholesterol, 99mg sodium, 280mg potassium.

Turkey with Beans

Preparation time: 10 minutes
Cooking time: 6 hours
Servings: 4

Ingredients:

- 1-pound turkey breasts, skinless, boneless and cut into strips
- 2 cups red kidney beans, boiled
- ¼ cup of water
- 1 tablespoon avocado oil
- ½ teaspoon chili powder
- 1 tablespoon tarragon, chopped

Directions:

1. In your slow cooker, mix the turkey with the beans, water, and the other ingredients, toss, put the lid on and cook on Low for 6 hours.
2. Divide the mix between plates and serve.

per serving: 435 calories,40.3g protein, 61.8g carbohydrates, 3.4g fat, 14.8g fiber, 49mg cholesterol, 116mg sodium, 164mg potassium.

Coriander Chicken

Preparation time: 10 minutes
Cooking time: 6 hours
Servings: 4

Ingredients:

- 1-pound chicken breasts, skinless, boneless, and cubed
- 1 tablespoon coriander, chopped
- ½ teaspoon turmeric powder
- 2 scallions, minced
- 1 tablespoon olive oil
- 1 tablespoon lime zest, grated
- ¼ cup lime juice
- 1 tablespoon chives, chopped

Directions:

1. In your slow cooker, mix the chicken with the coriander, turmeric, scallions, and the other ingredients, toss, put the lid on and cook on Low for 6 hours.
2. Divide the mix between plates and serve right away.

per serving: 250 calories,33g protein, 1g carbohydrates, 12g fat, 0.5g fiber, 101mg cholesterol, 99mg sodium, 309mg potassium.

Oregano and Turkey

Preparation time: 10 minutes
Cooking time: 6 hours
Servings: 4

Ingredients:

- 1 pound turkey breast, skinless, boneless, and cubed
- 1 tablespoon avocado oil
- ½ cup of water
- 2 tablespoons garlic, minced
- ½ teaspoon chili powder
- ½ teaspoon oregano, dried
- 1 tablespoon parsley, chopped

Directions:

1. In your slow cooker, mix the turkey with the oil, water, and the other ingredients, toss, put the lid on and cook on Low for 6 hours.
2. Divide the mix between plates and serve with a side salad.

per serving: 131 calories,19.8g protein, 6.7g carbohydrates, 2.4g fat, 1g fiber, 49mg cholesterol, 115mg sodium, 385mg potassium.

Cumin and Chives Chicken Mix

Preparation time: 10 minutes
Cooking time: 6 hours
Servings: 4

Ingredients:

- 1-pound chicken breast, skinless, boneless, and cubed
- 2 teaspoons olive oil
- 1 cup of water
- ½ teaspoon garam masala
- ½ teaspoon chili powder
- ½ teaspoon cumin, ground
- 1 yellow onion, chopped
- 1 tablespoon chives, chopped

Directions:

1. In your slow cooker, mix the chicken with the oil, water, and the other ingredients, toss, put the lid on and cook on Low for 6 hours.
2. Divide everything between plates and serve right away.

per serving: 163 calories,24.5g protein, 2.9g carbohydrates, 5.3g fat, 0.8g fiber, 73mg cholesterol, 65mg sodium, 474mg potassium.

Thyme Chicken

Preparation time: 10 minutes
Cooking time: 8 hours
Servings: 8

Ingredients:

- 2-pounds chicken fillet, chopped
- 1 garlic head, peeled
- 1 yellow onion, chopped
- 1 lemon, sliced
- 1 teaspoon thyme, dried
- 2 carrots, chopped

Directions:

3. Mix the chicken with half of the garlic and with half of the lemon slices and rub with salt, pepper, thyme, and paprika both outside and inside.
4. Put the carrots on the bottom of your Slow cooker, add the rest of the garlic, onion, and lemon slices, place the chicken on top, cover and cook on Low for 8 hours.
5. Transfer chicken to a platter, carve and serve with a side salad.

per serving: 230 calories, 33.2g protein, 3.7g carbohydrates, 8.4g fat, 0.9g fiber, 101mg cholesterol, 109mg sodium, 357mg potassium.

Sage and Paprika Turkey Breast

Preparation time: 10 minutes
Cooking time: 8 hours
Servings: 10

Ingredients:

- 3 pounds turkey breast, skinless, boneless
- 3 sweet potatoes, cut into wedges
- 2 white onions, cut into wedges
- ½ cup dried cranberries
- 1/3 cup water
- 1 teaspoon onion powder
- 1 teaspoon garlic powder
- 1 teaspoon parsley flakes
- 1 teaspoon thyme, dried
- 1 teaspoon sage, dried
- 1 teaspoon paprika, dried

Directions:

1. Put the turkey breast in your Slow cooker, add sweet potatoes, onions, cranberries, water, parsley, garlic and onion powder, thyme, sage, paprika, toss, cover, and cook on Low for 8 hours.
2. Discard bone from turkey breast, slice meat, divide between plates and serve with the veggies, figs, cherries, and berries on the side.

per serving: 174 calories, 23.8g protein, 13.1g carbohydrates, 2.4g fat, 2.2g fiber, 59mg cholesterol, 138mg sodium, 587mg potassium.

Nutmeg Chicken Breasts

Preparation time: 10 minutes
Cooking time: 6 hours
Servings: 8

Ingredients:
- 2 red bell peppers, chopped
- 2-pound chicken breasts, skinless and boneless
- 4 garlic cloves, minced
- 1 yellow onion, chopped
- 2 teaspoons paprika
- 1 cup of water
- ¼ teaspoon nutmeg, ground

Directions:
1. In a bowl, mix bell peppers with chicken breasts, garlic, onion, paprika, and nutmeg, toss to coat, transfer everything to your Slow cooker, add water, cover and cook on Low for 6 hours.
2. Divide chicken and veggies between plates and serve.

per serving: 235 calories,33.4g protein, 4.4g carbohydrates, 8.6g fat, 0.9g fiber, 101mg cholesterol, 100mg sodium, 371mg potassium.

Turkey Breast with Berries

Preparation time: 10 minutes
Cooking time: 6 hours
Servings: 12

Ingredients:
- 6-pound turkey breast, skinless
- 4 cups cranberries, rinsed
- 3 apples, peeled, cored, and sliced
- ½ cup balsamic vinegar
- ½ cup of water

Directions:
1. Put the turkey breast in your Slow cooker, add cranberries, apple slices, black pepper, vinegar, and water, toss a bit, cover, and cook on Low for 6 hours.
2. Slice turkey breast and divide between plates, mash cranberries and apples a bit, add them on top of the meat, and serve right away.

per serving: 287 calories,38.9g protein, 20.7g carbohydrates, 3.9g fat, 3.8g fiber, 98mg cholesterol, 230mg sodium, 814mg potassium.

Carrots with Chicken and Garlic

Preparation time: 10 minutes
Cooking time: 6 hours
Servings: 6

Ingredients:

- 1.5-pound chicken fillet, chopped
- 5 thyme springs, chopped
- 2 celery stalks, chopped
- 3 garlic cloves, minced
- 2 carrots, chopped
- 1 yellow onion, chopped

Directions:

1. Put half of the thyme, garlic, celery, onion, and carrots in your Slow cooker, add the chicken on top, and season with a pinch of white pepper.
2. Add the rest of the thyme, onion, garlic, celery, and carrots on top, cover, and cook on Low for 6 hours.
3. Divide chicken between plates and serve.

per serving: 234 calories,33.3g protein, 4.4g carbohydrates, 8.4g fat, 1g fiber, 101mg cholesterol, 117mg sodium, 388mg potassium.

Mediterranean Rosemary Chicken

Preparation time: 10 minutes
Cooking time: 4 hours
Servings: 5

Ingredients:

- 1 ½ pounds chicken breast, skinless and boneless
- Juice of 2 lemons
- 1 rosemary spring, chopped
- ¼ cup olive oil
- 3 garlic cloves, minced
- 1 cucumber, chopped
- ¼ cup red onions, chopped
- 2 tablespoons red vinegar

Directions:

1. In your Slow cooker, mix chicken with lemon juice, rosemary, oil, garlic, stir, cover, and cook on High for 4 hours.
2. Transfer chicken to a cutting board, shred with 2 forks, transfer to a bowl, add onion and vinegar, toss, divide between plates and serve.

per serving: 247 calories,20.9g protein, 1.1g carbohydrates, 13.5g fat, 0.2g fiber, 87mg cholesterol, 70mg sodium, 520mg potassium.

Sweet Potato and Chicken Chowder

Preparation time: 10 minutes
Cooking time: 6 hours
Servings: 5

Ingredients:

- 3 chicken breasts, skinless and boneless and cubed
- 4 cups of water
- 1 sweet potato, cubed
- 8 ounces green chilies, chopped
- 1 yellow onion, chopped
- 15 ounces coconut cream
- 1 teaspoon garlic powder
- 1 tablespoon parsley, chopped

Directions:

1. In your Slow cooker, mix chicken with stock, sweet potato, green chilies, onion, garlic powder, salt, and pepper, stir, cover, and cook on Low for 5 hours and 40 minutes.
2. Add coconut cream and parsley, stir, cover and cook on Low for 20 minutes more.
3. Ladle chowder into bowls.

per serving: 541 calories,32.9g protein, 43.6g carbohydrates, 29.5g fat, 16.2g fiber, 78mg cholesterol, 145mg sodium, 143mg potassium.

Ginger and Cumin Chicken Thighs

Preparation time: 10 minutes
Cooking time: 6 hours
Servings: 6

Ingredients:

- 2 pounds chicken thighs, boneless and skinless
- 1 yellow onion, chopped
- 3 carrots, chopped
- 3 garlic cloves, minced
- 2 teaspoons sweet paprika
- 1 teaspoon cinnamon, ground
- 2 teaspoons cumin, ground
- 2 teaspoons ginger, grated
- 1 cup of water

Directions:

1. In your Slow cooker, mix chicken with onion, carrots, garlic, paprika, cinnamon, cumin, ginger, water, stir, cover, and cook on Low for 6 hours.
2. Divide between plates, sprinkle cilantro on top, and serve.

per serving: 317 calories,44.6g protein, 6.6g carbohydrates, 11.5g fat, 1.8g fiber, 135mg cholesterol, 155mg sodium, 537mg potassium.

Chicken and Cilantro Mix

Preparation time: 10 minutes
Cooking time: 5 hours
Servings: 4

Ingredients:

- 1-pound chicken breast, skinless, boneless, and sliced
- 1 cup broccoli florets
- ½ cup tomato sauce, low sodium
- ½ cup chicken stock, low sodium
- 1 tablespoon avocado oil
- 1 yellow onion, sliced
- 3 garlic cloves, minced
- 1 tablespoon cilantro, chopped

Directions:

1. In your slow cooker, mix the chicken with the broccoli, tomato sauce, and the other ingredients, toss, put the lid on and cook on High for 5 hours.
2. Divide the mix between plates and serve hot.

per serving: 165 calories,25.7g protein, 6.8g carbohydrates, 3.5g fat, 1.9g fiber, 73mg cholesterol, 323mg sodium, 656mg potassium.

Snacks and Appetizers

Spinach and Cheese Spread

Preparation time: 10 minutes
Cooking time: 2 hours
Servings: 4

Ingredients:

- 4 ounces baby spinach
- 2 tablespoons Greek-style yogurt
- 2 ounces coconut cream
- ½ teaspoon turmeric powder
- 1 ounce Swiss cheese, shredded

Directions:

1. In your slow cooker, mix the spinach with the cream, yogurt, and the other ingredients, toss, put the lid on and cook on Low for 2 hours.
2. Divide into bowls and serve as a party spread.

per serving: 70 calories,3.2g protein, 2.7g carbohydrates, 5.7g fat, 1g fiber, 7mg cholesterol, 39mg sodium, 208mg potassium

Artichoke and Coconut Cream Dip

Preparation time: 10 minutes
Cooking time: 2 hours
Servings: 2

Ingredients:

- 2 oz artichoke hearts, boiled, chopped
- 2 ounces coconut cream
- ¼ cup mozzarella, shredded
- 2 green onions, chopped
- ½ teaspoon garam masala
- Cooking spray

Directions:

1. Grease your slow cooker with the cooking spray, and mix the artichokes with the cream, and the other ingredients inside.
2. Stir, cover, cook on Low for 2 hours, divide into bowls and serve as a party dip.

per serving: 93 calories,2.9g protein, 5.8g carbohydrates, 7.5G fat, 2.5g fiber, 2mg cholesterol, 56mg sodium, 221mg potassium

Crab and Green Onions Dip

Preparation time: 10 minutes
Cooking time: 1 hour
Servings: 6

Ingredients:
- 2 ounces crabmeat
- 1 tablespoon lime zest, grated
- ½ tablespoon lime juice
- 2 green onions, chopped
- 2 ounces cream cheese, low sodium
- Cooking spray

Directions:
1. Grease your slow cooker with the cooking spray, and mix the crabmeat with the lime zest, juice, and the other ingredients inside.
2. Put the lid on, cook on Low for 1 hour, divide into bowls, and serve as a party dip.

per serving: 40 calories, 2g protein, 1g carbohydrates, 3.3g fat, 0.2g fiber, 19mg cholesterol, 96mg sodium, 27mg potassium

Lemon Shrimp and Mozzarella Dip

Preparation time: 10 minutes
Cooking time: 2 hours
Servings: 6

Ingredients:
- 3 ounces cream cheese, low-sodium
- ½ cup coconut cream
- 1 pound shrimp, peeled, deveined, and chopped
- ½ tablespoon balsamic vinegar
- ½ tablespoon lemon juice
- 2 ounces mozzarella, shredded
- 1 tablespoon parsley, chopped

Directions:
1. In your slow cooker, mix the cream cheese with the shrimp, coconut cream, and the other ingredients, whisk, put the lid on and cook on Low for 2 hours.
2. Divide into bowls and serve as a dip.

per serving: 175 calories,20.9g protein, 3g carbohydrates, 8.6g fat, 0.5g fiber, 167mg cholesterol, 47mg sodium, 187mg potassium

Squash and Chives Salsa

Preparation time: 10 minutes
Cooking time: 3 hours
Servings: 6

Ingredients:

- 1 cup butternut squash, peeled and cubed
- 1 cup cherry tomatoes, cubed
- 1 cup avocado, peeled, pitted, and cubed
- ½ tablespoon balsamic vinegar
- ½ tablespoon lemon juice
- 1 tablespoon lemon zest, grated
- ¼ cup vegetable stock, low sodium
- 1 tablespoon chives, chopped

Directions:

1. In your slow cooker, mix the squash with the tomatoes, avocado, and the other ingredients, toss, put the lid on and cook on Low for 3 hours.
2. Divide into bowls and serve as a snack.

per serving: 67 calories, 1g protein, 6.3g carbohydrates, 4.8g fat, 2.6g fiber, 0mg cholesterol, 6mg sodium, 278mg potassium

Classic Beans Spread

Preparation time: 10 minutes
Cooking time: 6 hours
Servings: 4

Ingredients:

- 1 cup black beans, boiled
- ½ teaspoon balsamic vinegar
- ¼ cup vegetable stock
- ½ tablespoon olive oil

Directions:

1. In your slow cooker, mix the beans with all ingredients, toss, put the lid on and cook on Low for 6 hours.
2. Transfer to your food processor, blend well, divide into bowls, and serve.

per serving: 182 calories, 10.5g protein, 30.5g carbohydrates, 2.4g fat, 7.4g fiber, 0mg cholesterol, 11mg sodium, 728mg potassium

Rice and Spinach Snack Bowls

Preparation time: 10 minutes
Cooking time: 6 hours
Servings: 4

Ingredients:

- 1 red onion, sliced
- ½ cup of brown rice
- 2 cups vegetable stock, low sodium
- ½ cup baby spinach
- ½ cup cherry tomatoes halved
- 2 tablespoons pine nuts, toasted
- 1 tablespoon chives, chopped
- 1 tablespoon dill, chopped
- ½ tablespoon olive oil

Directions:

1. In your slow cooker, mix the rice with the onion, stock, and the other ingredients, toss, put the lid on, and cook on Low for 6 hours.
2. Divide into bowls and serve as a snack.

per serving: 162 calories, 3.2g protein, 26g carbohydrates, 5.5g fat, 1g fiber, 0mg cholesterol, 78mg sodium, 249mg potassium

Cauliflower and Mustard Spread

Preparation time: 10 minutes
Cooking time: 7 hours
Servings: 2

Ingredients:

- 1 cup cauliflower florets
- ½ cup coconut cream
- 1 tablespoon lemon juice
- ½ teaspoon garlic powder
- ¼ teaspoon ground paprika
- ¼ teaspoon mustard powder

Directions:

1. In your slow cooker, combine the cauliflower with the cream, and the other ingredients, toss, put the lid on, and cook on Low for 7 hours.
2. Transfer to a blender, pulse well, into bowls, and serve as a spread.

per serving: 157 calories, 2.7g protein, 6.9g carbohydrates, 14.6g fat, 2.8g fiber, 0mg cholesterol, 26mg sodium, 335mg potassium

Mushroom and Basil Dip

Preparation time: 10 minutes
Cooking time: 5 hours
Servings: 4

Ingredients:

- 4 ounces white mushrooms, chopped
- 1 eggplant, cubed
- ½ cup coconut cream
- ½ tablespoon olive oil
- 2 garlic cloves, minced
- 1 tablespoon balsamic vinegar
- ½ tablespoon basil, chopped
- ½ tablespoon oregano, chopped

Directions:

1. In your slow cooker, mix the mushrooms with the eggplant, cream, and the other ingredients, toss, put the lid on and cook on High for 5 hours.
2. Divide the mushroom mix into bowls and serve as a dip.

per serving: 124 calories, 2.9g protein, 10.2g carbohydrates, 9.3g fat, 5.3g fiber, 0mg cholesterol, 9mg sodium, 450mg potassium

Chickpeas and Garlic Spread

Preparation time: 10 minutes
Cooking time: 8 hours
Servings: 4

Ingredients:

- ½ cup chickpeas, boiled
- 1 tablespoon olive oil
- 1 tablespoon lemon juice
- 1 cup vegetable stock
- 1 garlic clove, minced
- ½ tablespoon chives, chopped

Directions:

1. In your slow cooker, combine the chickpeas with the stock, and the garlic, stir, put the lid on and cook on Low for 8 hours.
2. Drain chickpeas, transfer them to a blender, add the rest of the ingredients, pulse well, divide into bowls and serve as a party spread.

per serving: 128 calories, 5.2g protein, 16.5g carbohydrates, 5g fat, 4.7g fiber, 0mg cholesterol, 42mg sodium, 260mg potassium

Spinach and Garlic Dip

Preparation time: 10 minutes
Cooking time: 1 hour
Servings: 4

Ingredients:
- 2 tablespoons coconut cream
- ½ cup Greek yogurt
- ½ pound baby spinach
- 2 garlic cloves, minced

Directions:
1. In your slow cooker, mix the spinach with the cream and the other ingredients, toss, put the lid on and cook on High for 1 hour.
2. Blend using an immersion blender, divide into bowls and serve as a party dip.

per serving: 43 calories, 3.8g protein, 3.7g carbohydrates, 2g fat, 1.5g fiber, 0mg cholesterol, 54mg sodium, 342mg potassium

Sweet Potato Salad

Preparation time: 10 minutes
Cooking time: 8 hours
Servings: 3

Ingredients:
- 1 red onion, sliced
- 1 pound sweet potatoes, peeled and roughly cubed
- 2 tablespoons balsamic vinegar
- ½ cup coconut cream
- 1 tablespoon dill, chopped
- ½ cup celery, chopped

Directions:
1. In your slow cooker, mix the sweet potatoes with the cream, and the other ingredients, toss, put the lid on, and cook on Low for 8 hours.
2. Divide salad into bowls, and serve as an appetizer.

per serving: 292 calories, 4g protein, 49g carbohydrates, 9.9g fat, 8.3g fiber, 0mg cholesterol, 37mg sodium, 1478mg potassium

Stuffed Peppers

Preparation time: 10 minutes
Cooking time: 4 hours
Servings: 6

Ingredients:
- 1 red onion, chopped
- 1 teaspoon olive oil
- ½ teaspoon sweet paprika
- ½ tablespoon chili powder
- 1 garlic clove, minced
- 1 cup brown rice, cooked
- ½ cup of corn
- 2 bell peppers, tops, and insides scooped out
- ½ cup tomato sauce, low sodium

Directions:
1. In a bowl, mix the onion with the oil, paprika, and the other ingredients except for the peppers and tomato sauce, stir well and stuff the peppers with this mix.
2. Put the peppers in the slow cooker, add the sauce, put the lid on, and cook on Low for 4 hours.
3. Transfer the peppers on a platter and serve as an appetizer.

per serving: 160 calories,3.8g protein, 33g carbohydrates, 2.1g fat, 3g fiber, 0mg cholesterol, 118mg sodium, 307mg potassium

Corn and Mozzarella Dip

Preparation time: 10 minutes
Cooking time: 2 hours
Servings: 5

Ingredients:
- 1 cup of corn
- 1 tablespoon chives, chopped
- ½ cup coconut cream
- 2 ounces mozzarella, shredded
- ¼ teaspoon chili powder

Directions:
1. In your slow cooker, mix the corn with the chives and the other ingredients, whisk, put the lid on and cook on Low for 2 hours.
2. Divide into bowls and serve as a dip.

per serving: 114 calories,4.8g protein, 7.6g carbohydrates, 8.1g fat, 1.4g fiber, 6mg cholesterol, 78mg sodium, 151mg potassium

Tomato Salsa

Preparation time: 10 minutes
Cooking time: 4 hours
Servings: 2

Ingredients:
- 1 cup cherry tomatoes, halved
- 1 cup mushrooms, sliced
- 1 small yellow onion, chopped
- 1 garlic clove, minced
- 12 ounces tomato sauce, low sodium
- 1 tablespoon chives, chopped

Directions:
1. In your slow cooker, mix the tomatoes with the mushrooms and the other ingredients, toss, put the lid on and cook on Low for 4 hours.
2. Divide into bowls and serve as a party salsa

per serving: 40 calories,2.4g protein, 8.5g carbohydrates, 0.3g fat, 2.3g fiber, 0mg cholesterol, 8mg sodium, 386mg potassium

Green Onions and Beans Dip

Preparation time: 10 minutes
Cooking time: 1 hour
Servings: 4

Ingredients:
- ¼ cup salsa, low sodium
- 1 cup red kidney beans, cooked
- ½ cup mozzarella, shredded
- 1 tablespoon green onions, chopped

Directions:
1. In your slow cooker, mix the salsa with the beans and the other ingredients, toss, put the lid on cook on High for 1 hour.
2. Divide into bowls and serve as a party dip

per serving: 170 calories,11.6g protein, 29.5g carbohydrates, 1.2g fat, 7.3g fiber, 2mg cholesterol, 99mg sodium, 578mg potassium

Pineapple Salsa

Preparation time: 10 minutes
Cooking time: 6 hours
Servings: 4

Ingredients:

- ½ cup firm tofu, cubed
- 1 cup pineapple, peeled and cubed
- 1 cup cherry tomatoes, halved
- ½ tablespoons sesame oil
- ½ cup pineapple juice
- ½ tablespoon ginger, grated
- 1 garlic clove, minced

Directions:

1. In your slow cooker, mix the tofu with the pineapple and the other ingredients, toss, put the lid on and cook on Low for 6 hours.
2. Divide into bowls and serve as an appetizer.

per serving: 86 calories, 3.4g protein, 12.4g carbohydrates, 3.2g fat, 1.6g fiber, 0mg cholesterol, 7mg sodium, 251mg potassium

Chickpeas and Coriander Salsa

Preparation time: 10 minutes
Cooking time: 6 hours
Servings: 6

Ingredients:

- 1 cup chickpeas, cooked
- 1 cup vegetable stock, low sodium
- ½ cup black olives pitted and halved, fresh
- 1 small yellow onion, chopped
- ¼ tablespoon ginger, grated
- 4 garlic cloves, minced
- ¼ tablespoons coriander, ground
- ¼ tablespoons red chili powder
- ¼ tablespoons garam masala
- 1 tablespoon lemon juice

Directions:

1. In your slow cooker, mix the chickpeas with the stock, olives, and the other ingredients, toss, put the lid on and cook on Low for 6 hours.
2. Divide into bowls and serve as an appetizer.

per serving: 147 calories, 6.9g protein, 23.5g carbohydrates, 3.3g fat, 6.8g fiber, 0mg cholesterol, 114mg sodium, 330mg potassium

Mushroom Spread

Preparation time: 10 minutes
Cooking time: 4 hours
Servings: 6

Ingredients:
- 1 pound mushrooms, sliced
- 3 garlic cloves, minced
- 1 cup coconut cream
- 2 teaspoons ground paprika
- 2 tablespoons parsley, chopped

Directions:
1. In your slow cooker, mix the mushrooms with the garlic and the other ingredients, whisk, put the lid on and cook on Low for 4 hours.
2. Whisk, divide into bowls, and serve as a party spread.

per serving: 113 calories, 3.5g protein, 5.7g carbohydrates, 9.9g fat, 2g fiber, 0mg cholesterol, 12mg sodium, 375mg potassium

Bulgur Salsa

Preparation time: 10 minutes
Cooking time: 8 hours
Servings: 6

Ingredients:
- 1 cup vegetable stock, low sodium
- ½ cup bulgur
- 1 small yellow onion, chopped
- 1 red bell pepper, chopped
- 1 garlic clove, minced
- 5 ounces red kidney beans, cooked
- ½ cup of salsa
- 1 tablespoon chili powder
- ¼ teaspoon oregano, dried

Directions:
1. In your slow cooker, mix the bulgur with the stock and the other ingredients, toss, put the lid on and cook on Low for 8 hours.
2. Divide into bowls and serve cold as an appetizer.

per serving: 144 calories, 7.6g protein, 28.7g carbohydrates, 0.7g fat, 7.2g fiber, 0mg cholesterol, 172mg sodium, 515mg potassium

Beets and Nutmeg Salad

Preparation time: 10 minutes
Cooking time: 6 hours
Servings: 5

Ingredients:

- 2 cups beets, cubed
- ¼ cup carrots, grated
- 1 cup cherry tomatoes, halved
- ¼ cup vegetable stock, low sodium
- 3-ounce black beans, boiled
- ½ teaspoon nutmeg, ground
- ½ cup parsley, chopped

Directions:

1. In your slow cooker, mix the beets with the carrots, and the other ingredients, toss, put the lid on, and cook on Low for 6 hours.
2. Divide into bowls and serve cold as an appetizer.

per serving: 101 calories,5.4g protein, 20g carbohydrates, 0.6g fat, 4.8g fiber, 0mg cholesterol, 69mg sodium, 597mg potassium

Lentils and Sweet Onion Salsa

Preparation time: 10 minutes
Cooking time: 3 hours
Servings: 8

Ingredients:

- 1 cup lentils, boiled
- 1 cup mild salsa
- 3 ounces tomato paste, low sodium
- 2 tablespoons balsamic vinegar
- 1 small sweet onion, chopped
- 1 garlic clove, minced
- 1 tablespoon chives, chopped

Directions:

1. In your slow cooker, mix the lentils with the salsa and the other ingredients, toss, put the lid on and cook on High for 3 hours.
2. Divide into bowls and serve as a party salsa.

per serving: 107 calories,7.1g protein, 18.9g carbohydrates, 0.4g fat, 8.1g fiber, 0mg cholesterol, 101mg sodium, 355mg potassium

Cinnamon Tacos

Preparation time: 10 minutes
Cooking time: 4 hours
Servings: 4

Ingredients:
- 13 ounces pinto beans, cooked
- ¼ cup chili sauce, low sodium
- 2 ounces chipotle pepper, chopped
- ½ tablespoon cocoa powder
- ¼ teaspoon cinnamon powder
- 4 taco shells

Directions:
1. In your slow cooker, mix the beans with the chili sauce and the other ingredients except for the taco shells, toss, put the lid on and cook on Low for 4 hours.
2. Divide the mix into the taco shells and serve them as an appetizer.

per serving: 428 calories,21.7g protein, 72.8g carbohydrates, 7.2g fat, 15.7g fiber, 0mg cholesterol, 174mg sodium, 416mg potassium

Vanilla Almond Bowls

Preparation time: 10 minutes
Cooking time: 4 hours
Servings: 6

Ingredients:
- 1 tablespoon cinnamon powder
- 2 cups almonds
- ½ cup of water
- ½ teaspoons vanilla extract

Directions:
1. In your slow cooker, mix the almonds with the cinnamon and the other ingredients, toss, put the lid on and cook on Low for 4 hours.
2. Divide into bowls and serve as a snack.

per serving: 184 calories,6.7g protein, 6.8g carbohydrates, 15.8g fat, 4g fiber, 0mg cholesterol, 1mg sodium, 233mg potassium

Eggplant and Basil Salsa

Preparation time: 10 minutes
Cooking time: 7 hours
Servings: 5

Ingredients:
- 2 cups eggplant, chopped
- 1 teaspoon capers, chopped
- ½ cup of salsa
- 2 garlic cloves, minced
- ½ tablespoon basil, chopped
- 1 teaspoon balsamic vinegar

Directions:
1. In your slow cooker, mix the eggplant with the capers and the other ingredients, toss, put the lid on and cook on Low for 7 hours.
2. Divide into bowls and serve as an appetizer.

per serving: 17 calories,0.8g protein, 4g carbohydrates, 0.1g fat, 1.6g fiber, 0mg cholesterol, 174mg sodium, 159mg potassium

Easy Almond Spread

Preparation time: 10 minutes
Cooking time: 8 hours
Servings: 2

Ingredients:
- ¼ cup almonds
- 1 cup coconut cream

Directions:
1. In your slow cooker, mix the almonds with the cream, toss, put the lid on and cook on Low for 8 hours.
2. Transfer to a blender, pulse well, divide into bowls and serve.

per serving: 345 calories,5.3g protein, 9.2g carbohydrates, 34.6g fat, 4.1g fiber, 0mg cholesterol, 18mg sodium, 403mg potassium

Tender Onion Dip

Preparation time: 10 minutes
Cooking time: 8 hours
Servings: 4

Ingredients:
- 2 cups yellow onions, chopped
- 1 tablespoon olive oil
- ½ cup coconut cream

Directions:
1. In your slow cooker, mix the onions with the cream and the other ingredients, whisk, put the lid on and cook on Low for 8 hours.
2. Divide into bowls and serve as a party dip.

per serving: 122 calories,1.3g protein, 7g carbohydrates, 10.7g fat, 1.9g fiber, 0mg cholesterol, 7mg sodium, 163mg potassium

Nuts and Cream Bowls

Preparation time: 10 minutes
Cooking time: 2 hours
Servings: 2

Ingredients:
- 2 tablespoons almonds, toasted
- 2 tablespoons pecans, halved and toasted
- 2 tablespoons hazelnuts, toasted and peeled
- ½ cup coconut cream
- 2 tablespoons olive oil

Directions:
1. In your slow cooker, mix the nuts with all ingredients, toss, put the lid on, cook on Low for 2 hours, divide into bowls, and serve as a snack.

per serving: 419 calories,4.8g protein, 7.4g carbohydrates, 44.1g fat, 4.0g fiber, 0mg cholesterol, 9mg sodium, 291mg potassium

Eggplant and Cumin Salad

Preparation time: 10 minutes
Cooking time: 8 hours
Servings: 4

Ingredients:
- 2 eggplants, cubed
- 2 scallions, chopped
- 1 red bell pepper, chopped
- ½ teaspoon coriander, ground
- ½ cup of salsa
- 1 teaspoon cumin, ground
- 1 tablespoon lemon juice

Directions:
1. In your slow cooker, combine the eggplants with the scallions, pepper, and the other ingredients, toss, put the lid on, cook on Low for 8 hours, divide into bowls and serve cold as an appetizer salad.

per serving: 92 calories, 3.8g protein, 21.3g carbohydrates, 0.8g fat, 10.9g fiber, 0mg cholesterol, 204mg sodium, 815mg potassium

Lentils and Rosemary Dip

Preparation time: 10 minutes
Cooking time: 6 hours
Servings: 4

Ingredients:
- 2 carrots, peeled and grated
- 2 garlic cloves, minced
- 1 tablespoon olive oil
- ¼ cup lemon juice
- 1 cup lentils, cooked
- ½ tablespoon rosemary, chopped

Directions:
1. In your slow cooker, mix the lentils with the carrots, garlic, and the other ingredients, toss, put the lid on and cook on Low for 6 hours.
2. Transfer to a blender, pulse well, divide into bowls and serve.

per serving: 219 calories, 12.9g protein, 32.9g carbohydrates, 4.2g fat, 15.7g fiber, 0mg cholesterol, 27mg sodium, 585mg potassium

Turkey and Parsley Meatballs

Preparation time: 10 minutes
Cooking time: 7 hours
Servings: 6

Ingredients:

- 1-pound turkey breast, skinless, boneless, and ground
- 1 egg, whisked
- 6 ounces tomato puree, low-sodium, fresh
- 2 tablespoons parsley, chopped
- 1 tablespoon oregano, chopped
- 1 garlic clove, minced
- 1 small yellow onion, chopped

Directions:

1. In a bowl, mix the meat with the egg, parsley, and the other ingredients except for the tomato puree, stir well and shape medium meatballs out of it.
2. Put the meatballs in the slow cooker, add the tomato puree, put the lid on, and cook on Low for 7 hours
3. Arrange the meatballs on a platter and serve as an appetizer.

per serving: 97 calories,14.1g protein, 5.1g carbohydrates, 2.1g fat, 1g fiber, 60mg cholesterol, 79mg sodium, 277mg potassium

Macadamia Nuts and Onion Snack

Preparation time: 10 minutes
Cooking time: 2 hours
Servings: 6

Ingredients:

- ½ pound macadamia nuts
- 1 tablespoon avocado oil
- ¼ cup of water
- ½ tablespoon chili powder
- ½ teaspoon oregano, dried
- ½ teaspoon onion powder

Directions:

1. In your slow cooker, mix the macadamia nuts with the oil and the other ingredients, toss, put the lid on, cook on Low for 2 hours, divide into bowls and serve as a snack.

per serving: 278 calories,3.1g protein, 5.9g carbohydrates, 29.1g fat, 3.6g fiber, 0mg cholesterol, 9mg sodium, 163mg potassium

Turmeric Salmon Bites

Preparation time: 10 minutes
Cooking time: 2 hours
Servings: 6

Ingredients:

- 1 pound salmon fillets, boneless
- ¼ cup chili sauce
- ½ teaspoon turmeric powder
- 2 tablespoons grape jelly

Directions:

1. In your slow cooker, mix the salmon with the chili sauce and the other ingredients, toss gently, put the lid on, and cook on High for 2 hours.
2. Serve as an appetizer.

per serving: 120 calories,14.8g protein, 4.9g carbohydrates, 4.7g fat, 0.1g fiber, 33mg cholesterol, 89mg sodium, 314mg potassium

Paprika and Turmeric Cod Sticks

Preparation time: 10 minutes
Cooking time: 2 hours
Servings: 4

Ingredients:

- 1 egg, whisked
- ½ pound cod fillets, cut into medium strips
- ½ cup almond flour
- ½ teaspoon cumin, ground
- ½ teaspoon coriander, ground
- ½ teaspoon turmeric powder
- ¼ teaspoon ground paprika
- Cooking spray

Directions:

1. In a bowl, mix the flour with cumin, coriander, and the other ingredients except for the fish, eggs, and cooking spray.
2. Put the egg in another bowl and whisk it.
3. Dip the fish sticks in the egg and then dredge them in the flour mix.
4. Grease the slow cooker with cooking spray, add fish sticks, put the lid on, cook on High for 2 hours, arrange on a platter, and serve.

per serving: 86 calories,12.5g protein, 1.2g carbohydrates, 3.6g fat, 0.5g fiber, 74mg cholesterol, 55mg sodium, 32mg potassium

Walnuts Dip

Preparation time: 10 minutes
Cooking time: 2 hours
Servings: 4

Ingredients:
- ½ cup coconut cream
- ½ cup walnuts, chopped
- 1 cup baby spinach
- 1 garlic clove, chopped
- 1 tablespoon mayonnaise

Directions:
1. In your slow cooker, mix the spinach with the walnuts and the other ingredients, toss, put the lid on and cook on High for 2 hours.
2. Blend using an immersion blender, divide into bowls and serve as a party dip.

per serving: 183 calories,4.7g protein, 4.6g carbohydrates, 17.6g fat, 1.9g fiber, 1mg cholesterol, 37mg sodium, 206mg potassium

Curry Meatballs

Preparation time: 10 minutes
Cooking time: 4 hours
Servings: 4

Ingredients:
- 8 oz chicken fillet, sliced
- 1 red onion, chopped
- 1 egg, whisked
- 1 tablespoon cilantro, chopped
- 5 ounces of coconut milk
- ¼ tablespoon green curry paste

Directions:
1. In a bowl, mix the chicken with the onion and the other ingredients except for the coconut milk, stir well and shape medium meatballs out of this mix.
2. Put the meatballs in your slow cooker, add the coconut milk, put the lid on, and cook on High for 4 hours.
3. Arrange the meatballs on a platter and serve them as an appetizer

per serving: 219 calories,18.9g protein, 4.9g carbohydrates, 14g fat, 1.4g fiber, 91mg cholesterol, 108mg sodium, 287mg potassium

Paprika Calamari Rings

Preparation time: 10 minutes
Cooking time: 6 hours
Servings: 6

Ingredients:

- ½ pound calamari rings
- 1 tablespoon balsamic vinegar
- 1 cup vegetable stock, low sodium
- ½ teaspoon turmeric powder
- ½ teaspoon ground paprika
- ½ cup chicken stock

Directions:

1. In your slow cooker, mix the calamari rings with the vinegar, and the other ingredients, toss, put the lid on and cook on High for 6 hours.
2. Divide into bowls and serve right away as an appetizer.

per serving: 12 calories,1.6g protein, 0.8g carbohydrates, 0.2g fat, 0.3g fiber, 21mg cholesterol, 124mg sodium, 12mg potassium

Oregano and Basil Shrimp Salad

Preparation time: 10 minutes
Cooking time: 2 hours
Servings: 8

Ingredients:

- ½ pound shrimp, peeled and deveined
- 1 green bell pepper, chopped
- 4 spring onions, chopped
- 1 red bell pepper, chopped
- ½ cup of salsa
- 1 tablespoon olive oil
- 1 garlic clove, minced
- ¼ teaspoon oregano, dried
- ¼ teaspoon basil, dried
- 1 tablespoon parsley, chopped

Directions:

1. In your slow cooker, mix the shrimp with the peppers and the other ingredients, toss, put the lid on and cook on High for 2 hours.
2. Divide into bowls and serve as an appetizer.

per serving: 61 calories,7g protein, 3.3g carbohydrates, 2.3g fat, 0.7g fiber, 60mg cholesterol, 69mg sodium, 150mg potassium

Chicken and Chili Pepper Salad

Preparation time: 10 minutes
Cooking time: 6 hours
Servings: 7

Ingredients:

- 2 chicken breasts, skinless, boneless, and cubed
- ½ cup mild salsa
- ½ tablespoon olive oil
- 1 red onion, chopped
- ½ cup mushrooms, sliced
- ½ cup cherry tomatoes halved
- 1 chili pepper, chopped
- 2 ounces baby spinach
- 1 teaspoon oregano, chopped
- ½ tablespoon lemon juice
- ½ cup vegetable stock, low sodium

Directions:

1. In your slow cooker, mix the chicken with the salsa, oil, and the other ingredients except for the spinach, toss, put the lid on and cook on High for 5 hours. Add the spinach, cook on High for 1 more hour, divide into bowls and serve as an appetizer.

per serving: 106 calories,13g protein, 3.7g carbohydrates, 4.3g fat, 1g fiber, 37mg cholesterol, 156mg sodium, 222mg potassium

Apple Dip

Preparation time: 10 minutes
Cooking time: 6 hours
Servings: 8

Ingredients:

- 2 cups apples, peeled, cored, and chopped
- 1 cup carrots, peeled and grated
- ¼ teaspoon cloves, ground
- ¼ teaspoon ginger powder
- 1 tablespoon lemon juice
- ½ tablespoon lemon zest, grated
- ½ cup coconut cream
- ¼ teaspoon nutmeg, ground

Directions:

1. In your slow cooker, mix the apples with the carrots, cloves, and the other ingredients, toss, put the lid on and cook on Low for 6 hours.
2. Blend using an immersion blender, divide into bowls and serve.

per serving: 71 calories,0.6g protein, 10.1g carbohydrates, 3.7g fat, 2.1g fiber, 0mg cholesterol, 13mg sodium, 148mg potassium

Sweet Potato and Lemon Juice Dip

Preparation time: 10 minutes
Cooking time: 4 hours
Servings: 8

Ingredients:

- 2 sweet potatoes, peeled and cubed
- ½ cup coconut cream
- ½ teaspoon turmeric powder
- ½ teaspoon garam masala
- 2 garlic cloves, minced
- ½ cup vegetable stock, low sodium
- 1 cup basil leaves
- 2 tablespoons olive oil
- 1 tablespoon lemon juice

Directions:

1. In your slow cooker, mix the sweet potatoes with the cream, turmeric, and the other ingredients, toss, put the lid on and cook on High for 4 hours.
2. Blend using an immersion blender, divide into bowls and serve as a party dip.

per serving: 90 calories,0.8g protein, 6.7g carbohydrates, 7.2g fat, 1.3g fiber, 0mg cholesterol, 14mg sodium, 210mg potassium

Spinach and Calamari Salad

Preparation time: 10 minutes
Cooking time: 4 hours and 30 minutes
Servings: 6

Ingredients:

- 2 cups baby spinach
- ½ cup walnuts, chopped
- ½ cup mild salsa
- 1 cup calamari rings
- ½ teaspoons thyme, chopped
- 2 garlic cloves, minced
- 1 cup tomatoes, cubed
- ¼ cup vegetable stock, low sodium

Directions:

1. In your slow cooker, mix the salsa with the calamari rings and the other ingredients except for the spinach, toss, put the lid on and cook on High for 4 hours.
2. Add the spinach, toss, put the lid on, cook on High for 30 minutes more, divide into bowls, and serve.

per serving: 93 calories,6.4g protein, 4g carbohydrates, 6.5g fat, 1.4g fiber, 43mg cholesterol, 208mg sodium, 186mg potassium

Fragrant Meatballs

Preparation time: 10 minutes
Cooking time: 7 hours
Servings: 7

Ingredients:
- ½ pound chicken breast, skinless, boneless, ground
- 1 egg, whisked
- ½ cup salsa Verde
- 1 teaspoon oregano, dried
- ½ teaspoon chili powder
- ½ teaspoon rosemary, dried
- 1 tablespoon parsley, chopped

Directions:
1. In a bowl, mix the chicken with the egg and the other ingredients except for the salsa, stir well and shape medium meatballs out of this mix.
2. Put the meatballs in the slow cooker, add the salsa Verde, toss gently, put the lid on and cook on Low for 7 hours.
3. Arrange the meatballs on a platter and serve.

per serving: 52 calories,7.9g protein, 1.1g carbohydrates, 1.5g fat, 0.3g fiber, 44mg cholesterol, 126mg sodium, 139mg potassium

Pecans Snack

Preparation time: 10 minutes
Cooking time: 3 hours
Servings: 10

Ingredients:
- ½ tablespoon cinnamon powder
- ¼ cup of water
- ½ tablespoon avocado oil
- ½ teaspoon chili powder
- 2 cups pecans

Directions:
1. In your slow cooker, mix the pecans with the cinnamon and the other ingredients, toss, put the lid on and cook on Low for 3 hours.
2. Divide the pecans into bowls and serve as a snack.

per serving: 118 calories,1.8g protein, 2.5g carbohydrates, 12.1g fat, 1.9g fiber, 0mg cholesterol, 2mg sodium, 74mg potassium

Cajun Almonds and Seafood Bowls

Preparation time: 10 minutes
Cooking time: 2 hours
Servings: 8

Ingredients:
- 1 cup almonds
- 1 pound shrimp, peeled and deveined
- ½ cup mild salsa
- ½ tablespoon Cajun seasoning

Directions:
1. In your slow cooker, mix the shrimp with the almonds, and the other ingredients, toss, put the lid on and cook on High for 2 hours.
2. Divide between small plates and serve as an appetizer.

per serving: 140 calories,15.6g protein, 4.1g carbohydrates, 6.9g fat, 1.5g fiber, 119mg cholesterol, 37mg sodium, 183mg potassium

Desserts

Aromatic Apples

Preparation time: 10 minutes
Cooking time: 2 hours
Servings: 2

Ingredients:

- 2 tablespoons honey
- 1 tablespoon ground cinnamon
- 2 tablespoons walnuts, chopped
- A pinch of nutmeg, ground
- ½ tablespoon lemon juice
- ¼ cup of water
- 2 apples, cored and tops cut off

Directions:

1. In your slow cooker, mix the apples with the honey, cinnamon, and the other ingredients, toss, put the lid on and cook on High for 2 hours.
2. Divide the mix between plates and serve.

per serving: 237 calories, 2.7g protein, 51.7g carbohydrates, 5.7g fat, 7.8g fiber, 0mg cholesterol, 5mg sodium, 310mg potassium.

Honey Pears

Preparation time: 10 minutes
Cooking time: 2 hours
Servings: 2

Ingredients:

- 2 tablespoons avocado oil
- 1 teaspoon vanilla extract
- 2 pears, cored and halved
- ½ tablespoon lime juice
- 1 tablespoon honey

Directions:

1. In your slow cooker combine the pears with the honey, oil, and the other ingredients, toss, put the lid on and cook on High for 2 hours.
2. Divide between plates and serve.

per serving: 179 calories, 1g protein, 42.1g carbohydrates, 2.1g fat, 7.1g fiber, 0mg cholesterol, 5mg sodium, 301mg potassium.

Almond Cake

Preparation time: 10 minutes
Cooking time: 2 hours
Servings: 4

Ingredients:

- ½ cup honey
- 2 tablespoons coconut oil, melted
- 1 cup avocado, peeled and mashed
- ½ teaspoon vanilla extract
- 1 egg
- ½ teaspoon baking powder
- 1 cup almond flour
- ¼ cup organic almond milk
- Cooking spray

Directions:

1. In a bowl, mix the honey with the oil, avocado, and the other ingredients except for the cooking spray and whisk well.
2. Grease your slow cooker with cooking spray, add the cake batter, spread, put the lid on, and cook on High for 2 hours.
3. Leave the cake to cool down, slice, and serve.

per serving: 322 calories, 3.8g protein, 40.1g carbohydrates, 18.7g fat, 3.4g fiber, 41mg cholesterol, 32mg sodium, 282mg potassium.

Honey Coconut Cream

Preparation time: 10 minutes
Cooking time: 1 hour
Servings: 2

Ingredients:

- 2 ounces coconut cream
- 1 cup of coconut milk
- ½ teaspoon almond extract
- 2 tablespoons honey

Directions:

1. In your slow cooker, mix the cream with the milk and the other ingredients, whisk, put the lid on, cook on High for 1 hour, divide into bowls, and serve cold.

per serving: 219 calories, 1.9g protein, 13.5g carbohydrates, 19.1g fat, 1.4g fiber, 0mg cholesterol, 9mg sodium, 167mg potassium.

Sweet Rice Pudding

Preparation time: 10 minutes
Cooking time: 1 hour
Servings: 4

Ingredients:
- 2 tablespoons almonds, chopped
- 1 cup of brown rice
- 2 cups organic almond milk
- 1 tablespoon honey
- ¼ teaspoon ground cinnamon
- ¼ teaspoon ginger, grated

Directions:
1. In your slow cooker, mix the coconut milk with the rice, honey, and the other ingredients, toss, put the lid on and cook on High for 1 hour.
2. Divide the pudding into bowls and serve cold

per serving: 482 calories, 7g protein, 48g carbohydrates, 31.4g fat, 4.7g fiber, 0mg cholesterol, 20mg sodium, 469mg potassium.

Cherry Bowls with Syrup

Preparation time: 10 minutes
Cooking time: 1 hour
Servings: 4

Ingredients:
- 1 cup cherries, pitted
- 1 tablespoon honey
- ½ cup red cherry juice
- 2 tablespoons maple syrup

Directions:
1. In your slow cooker, mix the cherries with the honey and the other ingredients, toss gently, put the lid on, cook on High for 1 hour, divide into bowls and serve.

per serving: 80 calories, 0.5g protein, 19.4g carbohydrates, 0g fat, 0.8g fiber, 0mg cholesterol, 5mg sodium, 23mg potassium.

Coconut Berry Cream

Preparation time: 10 minutes
Cooking time: 2 hours
Servings: 2

Ingredients:

- 2 tablespoons cashews, chopped
- 1 cup of coconut milk
- ½ cup blueberries
- ½ cup maple syrup
- ½ tablespoon coconut oil, melted

Directions:

1. In your slow cooker, mix the coconut milk with the berries and the other ingredients, whisk, put the lid on and cook on Low for 2 hours.
2. Divide the mix into bowls and serve cold.

per serving: 581 calories,4.4g protein, 67.5g carbohydrates, 36.3g fat, 3.8g fiber, 0mg cholesterol, 27mg sodium, 553mg potassium.

Lemon Maple Pudding

Preparation time: 10 minutes
Cooking time: 1 hour
Servings: 4

Ingredients:

- ¼ cup cashew butter
- 1 tablespoon coconut oil, melted
- ½ cup of brown rice
- 1 cup organic almond milk
- 2 tablespoons lemon juice
- ½ teaspoon lemon zest, grated
- 1 tablespoon honey

Directions:

1. In your slow cooker, mix the rice with the milk, coconut oil, and the other ingredients, whisk, put the lid on and cook on High for 1 hour.
2. Divide into bowls and serve.

per serving: 365 calories,6.1g protein, 30.4g carbohydrates, 26.3g fat, 2.5g fiber, 0mg cholesterol, 14mg sodium, 322mg potassium.

Cinnamon Orange Pudding

Preparation time: 10 minutes
Cooking time: 1 hour
Servings: 4

Ingredients:

- 1 tablespoon chia seeds
- ½ cup organic organic organic almond milk
- ½ cup oranges, peeled and cut into segments
- 1 tablespoon honey
- ½ teaspoon ground cinnamon
- 1 tablespoon coconut oil, melted
- 2 tablespoons pecans, chopped

Directions:

1. In your slow cooker, mix the chia seeds with the organic almond milk, orange segments, and the other ingredients, toss, put the lid on and cook on High for 1 hour.
2. Divide the pudding into bowls and serve cold.

per serving: 209 calories,2.9g protein, 12.8g carbohydrates, 17.8g fat, 4.6g fiber, 0mg cholesterol, 6mg sodium, 181mg potassium.

Creamy Berries

Preparation time: 10 minutes
Cooking time: 1 hour
Servings: 2

Ingredients:

- ½ teaspoon nutmeg, ground
- ½ teaspoon vanilla extract
- ½ cup blackberries
- ½ cup blueberries
- ¼ cup coconut cream
- 1 tablespoon honey
- 2 tablespoons walnuts, chopped

Directions:

1. In your slow cooker, combine the berries with the cream and the other ingredients, toss gently, put the lid on, cook on High for 1 hour, divide into bowls, and serve.

per serving: 191 calories,3.4g protein, 20.2g carbohydrates, 13.3g fat, 4.1g fiber, 0mg cholesterol, 6mg sodium, 215mg potassium.

Plums Saute

Preparation time: 10 minutes
Cooking time: 1 hour
Servings: 4

Ingredients:

- 1 pound plums, pitted and halved
- ½ teaspoon nutmeg, ground
- 1 cup of water
- 1 ½ tablespoon honey
- 1 tablespoon vanilla extract

Directions:

1. In your slow cooker, mix the plums with the water and the other ingredients, toss gently, put the lid on, and cook on High for 1 hour.
2. Divide the mix into bowls and serve.

per serving: 42 calories,0.2g protein, 9g carbohydrates, 0.2g fat, 0.3g fiber, 0mg cholesterol, 2mg sodium, 36mg potassium.

Vanilla Peach Mix

Preparation time: 10 minutes
Cooking time: 2 hours
Servings: 2

Ingredients:

- 2 cups peaches, peeled and halved
- 3 tablespoons honey
- ½ teaspoon ground cinnamon
- ½ cup coconut cream
- 1 teaspoon vanilla extract

Directions:

1. In your slow cooker, mix the peaches with the honey and the other ingredients, toss, put the lid on and cook on High for 2 hours.
2. Divide the mix into bowls and serve.

per serving: 300 calories,2.9g protein, 44g carbohydrates, 14.7g fat, 4g fiber, 0mg cholesterol, 11mg sodium, 465mg potassium.

Delightful Pears Mix

Preparation time: 10 minutes
Cooking time: 2 hours
Servings: 2

Ingredients:
- 2 pears, peeled and cored
- 1 cup apple juice
- ½ tablespoon honey
- 1 tablespoon ginger, grated

Directions:
1. In your slow cooker, mix the pears with the apple juice and the other ingredients, toss, put the lid on and cook on Low for 2 hours.
2. Divide the mix into bowls and serve warm.

per serving: 203 calories, 1.1g protein, 52.1g carbohydrates, 0.6g fat, 7.1g fiber, 0mg cholesterol, 9mg sodium, 406mg potassium.

Honey Cookies

Preparation time: 10 minutes
Cooking time: 2 hours and 30 minutes
Servings: 5

Ingredients:
- 1 tablespoon coconut oil, melted
- 2 eggs, whisked
- ¼ cup honey
- ½ cup raisins
- ¼ cup organic almond milk
- ¼ teaspoon vanilla extract
- ¼ teaspoon baking powder
- 1 cup almond flour

Directions:
1. In a bowl, mix the eggs with the raisins, organic almond milk, and the other ingredients and whisk well.
2. Line your slow cooker with parchment paper, spread the cookie mix on the bottom of the pot, put the lid on, cook on Low for 2 hours and 30 minutes, leave aside to cool down, cut with a cookie cutter, and serve.

per serving: 306 calories, 7.8g protein, 31.2g carbohydrates, 18g fat, 3.2g fiber, 65mg cholesterol, 37mg sodium, 198mg potassium.

Blueberries Confitur

Preparation time: 10 minutes
Cooking time: 4 hours
Servings: 2

Ingredients:
- 2 cups blueberries
- ½ cup of water
- ¼ pound honey
- Zest of 1 lime

Directions:
1. In your slow cooker, combine the berries with the water and the other ingredients, toss, put the lid on and cook on High for 4 hours.
2. Divide into small jars and serve cold.

per serving: 266 calories,1.3g protein, 70.4g carbohydrates, 0.5g fat, 3.6g fiber, 0mg cholesterol, 5mg sodium, 142mg potassium.

Citrus Bowls

Preparation time: 10 minutes
Cooking time: 3 hours
Servings: 2

Ingredients:
- ½ pound oranges, peeled and cut into segments
- 1 cup coconut cream
- ½ tablespoon almonds, chopped
- 1 tablespoon chia seeds
- 1 tablespoon honey

Directions:
1. In your slow cooker, mix the oranges with the cream and the other ingredients, toss, put the lid on and cook on Low for 3 hours.
2. Divide into bowls and serve.

per serving: 439 calories,6.5g protein, 34.9g carbohydrates, 33.8g fat, 10.4g fiber, 0mg cholesterol, 21mg sodium, 595mg potassium.

Peach Cream

Preparation time: 10 minutes
Cooking time: 3 hours
Servings: 2

Ingredients:
- ¼ teaspoon ground cinnamon
- 1 cup peaches, pitted and chopped
- ¼ cup coconut cream
- Cooking spray
- 1 tablespoon maple syrup
- ½ teaspoons vanilla extract
- 2 tablespoons honey

Directions:
1. In a blender, mix the peaches with the cinnamon and the other ingredients except for the cooking spray and pulse well.
2. Grease the slow cooker with the cooking spray, pour the cream mix inside, put the lid on and cook on Low for 3 hours.
3. Divide the cream into bowls and serve cold.

per serving: 192 calories,1.5g protein, 33g carbohydrates, 7.4g fat, 2g fiber, 0mg cholesterol,6mg sodium, 256mg potassium.

Spiced Plums

Preparation time: 10 minutes
Cooking time: 2 hours
Servings: 2

Ingredients:
- ½ pound plums pitted and halved
- 2 tablespoons honey
- 1 teaspoon cinnamon, ground
- ½ cup of orange juice

Directions:
1. In your slow cooker, mix the plums with the cinnamon and the other ingredients, toss, put the lid on and cook on Low for 2 hours.
2. Divide into bowls and serve as a dessert.

per serving: 102 calories,0.7g protein, 26.7g carbohydrates, 0.2g fat, 1g fiber, 0mg cholesterol, 1mg sodium, 166mg potassium.

Aromatic and Tender Apples

Preparation time: 10 minutes
Cooking time: 2 hours
Servings: 2

Ingredients:

- 1 pound apples, cored and cut into wedges
- ½ cup organic almond milk
- ¼ teaspoon cardamom, ground
- 2 tablespoons honey

Directions:

1. In your slow cooker, mix the apples with the cardamom and the other ingredients, toss, put the lid on and cook on High for 2 hours.
2. Divide the mix into bowls and serve cold.

per serving: 138 calories,0.6g protein, 34.9g carbohydrates, 0.8g fat, 3.1g fiber, 0mg cholesterol, 39mg sodium, 178mg potassium.

Coconut Cream and Rhubarb Mix

Preparation time: 10 minutes
Cooking time: 2 hours
Servings: 2

Ingredients:

- 2 cups rhubarb, sliced
- ½ cup cherries pitted
- 1 tablespoon pumpkin puree
- ¼ cup coconut cream
- ½ cup of honey

Directions:

1. In your slow cooker, mix the rhubarb with the cherries and the other ingredients, toss, put the lid on and cook on High for 2 hours.
2. Divide the mix into bowls and serve cold.

per serving: 374 calories,2.5g protein, 82.4g carbohydrates, 7.5g fat, 3.9g fiber, 0mg cholesterol, 13mg sodium, 557mg potassium.

Peaches with Tender Grape Sauce

Preparation time: 10 minutes
Cooking time: 2 hours
Servings: 2

Ingredients:

- 3 tablespoons honey
- 1 pound peaches, pitted and cut into wedges
- ½ cup grape juice, fresh
- ½ teaspoon vanilla extract
- 1 teaspoon lemon zest, grated

Directions:

1. In your slow cooker, mix the peaches with the honey and the other ingredients, toss, put the lid on and cook on High for 2 hours.
2. Divide into bowls and serve.

per serving: 152 calories,1.1g protein, 38.8g carbohydrates, 0.3g fat, 1.3g fiber, 0mg cholesterol, 2mg sodium, 258mg potassium.

Apricot Cream

Preparation time: 10 minutes
Cooking time: 2 hours
Servings: 2

Ingredients:

- 1 cup apricots, pitted and chopped
- 1 cup peaches, pitted and chopped
- 1 cup coconut cream
- 3 tablespoons honey
- 1 teaspoon vanilla extract

Directions:

1. In a blender, mix the apricots with the peaches and the other ingredients, and pulse well.
2. Put the cream in the slow cooker, put the lid on, cook on High for 2 hours, divide into bowls, and serve.

per serving: 444 calories,4.5g protein, 48.4g carbohydrates, 29.3g fat, 5.4g fiber, 0mg cholesterol, 20mg sodium, 678mg potassium.

Grapes Mix

Preparation time: 10 minutes
Cooking time: 2 hours
Servings: 2

Ingredients:

- 1 cup grapes, halved
- ½ teaspoon vanilla extract
- 1 cup oranges, peeled and cut into segments
- ¼ cup of water
- 1 and ½ tablespoons honey
- 1 teaspoon lemon juice

Directions:

1. In your slow cooker, mix the grapes with the oranges, water, and the other ingredients, toss, put the lid on and cook on Low for 2 hours.
2. Divide into bowls and serve.

per serving: 125 calories,1.2g protein, 31.6g carbohydrates, 0.3g fat, 2.6g fiber, 0mg cholesterol, 3mg sodium, 264mg potassium.

Pomegranate Bowls

Preparation time: 10 minutes
Cooking time: 3 hours
Servings: 2

Ingredients:

- 2 cups pomegranate seeds
- 1 cup mango, peeled and cubed
- ½ cup coconut cream
- 1 tablespoon lemon juice
- ½ teaspoon vanilla extract
- 2 tablespoons honey

Directions:

1. In your slow cooker, combine the mango with the pomegranate seeds and the other ingredients, toss, put the lid on and cook on Low for 3 hours.
2. Divide into bowls and serve cold.

per serving: 195 calories, 2.1g protein, 17.3g carbohydrates, 14.7g fat, 2.7g fiber, 0mg cholesterol, 11mg sodium, 307mg potassium.

Tangerine Sweet Sauce

Preparation time: 10 minutes
Cooking time: 2 hours
Servings: 2

Ingredients:
- 1 tablespoon ginger, grated
- 3 tablespoons honey
- 3 tangerines, peeled and chopped
- 2 tablespoons agave nectar
- ½ cup coconut cream

Directions:
1. In your slow cooker, mix the ginger with the honey, mandarins, and the other ingredients, whisk, put the lid on and cook on High for 2 hours.
2. Blend the cream using an immersion blender, divide into bowls and serve cold.

per serving: 349 calories, 2.5g protein, 59.1g carbohydrates, 14.5g fat, 3.6g fiber, 0mg cholesterol, 17mg sodium, 376mg potassium.

Vanilla Berries Mash

Preparation time: 10 minutes
Cooking time: 1 hour
Servings: 4

Ingredients:
- 3 cups cranberries
- ½ cup of water
- ½ cup coconut cream
- ½ teaspoon vanilla extract
- ½ teaspoon almond extract
- ½ cup of honey

Directions:
1. In your slow cooker, mix the cranberries with the water, cream, and the other ingredients, whisk, put the lid on and cook on High for 1 hour.
2. Transfer to a blender, pulse well, divide into bowls and serve cold.

per serving: 244 calories, 0.8g protein, 44.2g carbohydrates, 7.2g fat, 3.7g fiber, 0mg cholesterol, 7mg sodium, 242mg potassium.

Strawberry Mix

Preparation time: 10 minutes
Cooking time: 1 hour
Servings: 2

Ingredients:

- 2 tablespoons honey
- 1 cup orange segments
- 1 cup strawberries, halved
- A pinch of ginger powder
- ½ teaspoon vanilla extract
- ½ cup of orange juice
- 1 tablespoon chia seeds

Directions:

1. In your slow cooker, mix the oranges with the berries, ginger powder, and the other ingredients, toss, put the lid on and cook on High for 1 hour.
2. Divide into bowls and serve cold.

per serving: 365 calories,8g protein, 59g carbohydrates, 12.2g fat, 16.2g fiber, 0mg cholesterol, 12mg sodium, 123mg potassium.

Sweet Plums and Mango

Preparation time: 10 minutes
Cooking time: 1 hour
Servings: 2

Ingredients:

- 2 teaspoons orange zest
- 1 tablespoon orange juice
- 1 cup plums, pitted and halved
- 1 cup mango, peeled and cubed
- 1 tablespoon maple syrup
- 3 tablespoons honey

Directions:

1. In your slow cooker, mix the plums with the mango and the other ingredients, toss, put the lid on and cook on High for 1 hour.
2. Divide into bowls and serve cold

per serving: 192 calories,1.1g protein, 50.3g carbohydrates, 0.5g fat, 2.1g fiber, 0mg cholesterol, 3mg sodium, 247mg potassium.

Aromatic Jam

Preparation time: 10 minutes
Cooking time: 3 hours
Servings: 2

Ingredients:
- ½ cup lemon juice
- 1 orange, peeled, and cut into segments
- 1 lemon, peeled and cut into segments
- ½ cup of water
- 2 tablespoons lemon zest, grated
- ¼ cup of honey
- A pinch of ground cinnamon

Directions:
1. In your slow cooker, mix the lemon juice with the honey, water, and the other ingredients, whisk, put the lid on and cook on Low for 3 hours.
2. Divide into small jars and serve cold.

per serving: 195 calories, 1.8g protein, 49.7g carbohydrates, 0.7g fat, 3.3g fiber, 0mg cholesterol, 16mg sodium, 305mg potassium.

Pear Butter

Preparation time: 10 minutes
Cooking time: 3 hours
Servings: 4

Ingredients:
- ½ pound pears, peeled and chopped
- ½ cup coconut cream
- ½ cup honey
- 1 tablespoon lemon zest, grated
- Juice of ½ lemon

Directions:
1. In your slow cooker, mix the pears with the cream and the other ingredients, whisk, put the lid on and cook on Low for 3 hours.
2. Blend using an immersion blender, divide into cups and serve cold.

per serving: 232 calories, 1.1g protein, 45.5g carbohydrates, 7.2g fat, 2.6g fiber, 0mg cholesterol, 7mg sodium, 171mg potassium.

Rhubarb Delight

Preparation time: 10 minutes
Cooking time: 2 hours
Servings: 2

Ingredients:
- ½ pound rhubarb, sliced
- ¼ cup of honey
- 1 tablespoon lemon juice
- 1 cup of water

Directions:
1. In your slow cooker, mix the rhubarb with the honey and the other ingredients, toss, put the lid on and cook on High for 2 hours.
2. Whisk the jam, divide into bowls and serve cold.

per serving: 154 calories,1.2g protein, 40.2g carbohydrates, 0.3g fat, 2.2g fiber, 0mg cholesterol, 11mg sodium, 359mg potassium.

Apricot Jam

Preparation time: 10 minutes
Cooking time: 3 hours
Servings: 8

Ingredients:
- 1 cup apricots, chopped
- ½ cup of water
- 1 teaspoon vanilla extract
- 2 tablespoons lemon juice
- 1 cup of honey

Directions:
1. In your slow cooker, mix the apricots with the water, vanilla, and the other ingredients, whisk, put the lid on and cook on High for 3 hours.
2. Stir the marmalade, divide into bowls and serve cold.

per serving: 269 calories,0.5g protein, 72.1g carbohydrates, 0.2g fat, 0.6g fiber, 0mg cholesterol, 5mg sodium, 100mg potassium.

Mango Mix

Preparation time: 10 minutes
Cooking time: 2 hours
Servings: 5

Ingredients:
- 1 cup mango, peeled and cubed
- 1 apple, cored and cubed
- 1 cup coconut cream
- 1 tablespoon lemon juice

Directions:
1. In your slow cooker, combine mango and the other ingredients, toss gently, put the lid on, and cook on Low for 2 hours.
2. Divide the mix into bowls and serve.

per serving: 239 calories, 2.1g protein, 23.3g carbohydrates, 17.4g fat, 4.7g fiber, 0mg cholesterol, 11mg sodium, 379mg potassium.

Peaches with Aromatic Sauce

Preparation time: 10 minutes
Cooking time: 2 hours
Servings: 2

Ingredients:
- 3 tablespoons water
- 1 pound peaches, pitted and cut into wedges
- ¼ cup grape juice
- ½ teaspoon ground cardamom
- 1 teaspoon lemon zest, grated

Directions:
1. In your slow cooker, mix the peaches with the water and the other ingredients, toss, put the lid on and cook on High for 2 hours.
2. Divide into bowls and serve.

per serving: 141 calories, 1g protein, 36.1g carbohydrates, 0.2g fat, 1.3g fiber, 0mg cholesterol, 2mg sodium, 211mg potassium.

Peaches Cream with Honey

Preparation time: 10 minutes
Cooking time: 2 hours
Servings: 3

Ingredients:
- 1 cup peaches, pitted and chopped
- 1 cup coconut cream
- 3 tablespoons honey

Directions:
1. In a blender, mix peaches and the other ingredients, and pulse well.
2. Put the cream in the slow cooker, put the lid on, cook on High for 2 hours, divide into bowls, and serve.

per serving: 296 calories,3g protein, 32.3g carbohydrates, 19.5g fat, 3.6g fiber, 0mg cholesterol, 14mg sodium, 452mg potassium.

Vanilla Mix with Grape

Preparation time: 10 minutes
Cooking time: 2 hours
Servings: 2

Ingredients:
- 1 cup grapes, halved
- ½ teaspoon vanilla extract
- 1 cup oranges, peeled and cut into segments
- ¼ cup of water
- 1 teaspoon lemon juice

Directions:
1. In your slow cooker, mix the grapes with the oranges, water, and the other ingredients, toss, put the lid on and cook on Low for 2 hours.
2. Divide into bowls and serve.

per serving: 125 calories,1.2g protein, 31.6g carbohydrates, 0.3g fat, 2.6g fiber, 0mg cholesterol, 3mg sodium, 264mg potassium.

Coconut Cream and Pomegranate Mix

Preparation time: 10 minutes
Cooking time: 3 hours
Servings: 3

Ingredients:
- 2 cups pomegranate seeds
- ½ cup coconut cream
- ½ teaspoon vanilla extract
- 2 tablespoons honey

Directions:
1. In your slow cooker, combine the mango with the pomegranate seeds and the other ingredients, toss, put the lid on and cook on Low for 3 hours.
2. Divide into bowls and serve cold.

per serving: 237 calories,2.1g protein, 38.2g carbohydrates, 9.8g fat, 2.5g fiber, 0mg cholesterol, 8mg sodium, 212mg potassium.

Mandarin Cream

Preparation time: 10 minutes
Cooking time: 2 hours
Servings: 3

Ingredients:
- 1 tablespoon ground cardamom
- 3 mandarins, peeled and chopped
- ½ cup coconut cream

Directions:
1. In your slow cooker, mix the ground cardamom with tangerines and the other ingredients, whisk, put the lid on and cook on High for 2 hours.
2. Blend the cream using an immersion blender, divide into bowls and serve cold.

per serving: 239 calories,1.7g protein, 40.8g carbohydrates,9.9g fat, 3.1g fiber, 0mg cholesterol, 9mg sodium, 256mg potassium.

Berries and Honey Mash

Preparation time: 10 minutes
Cooking time: 1 hour
Servings: 2

Ingredients:

- 3 cups cranberries
- ½ teaspoon vanilla extract
- 1 tablespoon honey

Directions:

1. In your slow cooker, mix the cranberries with vanilla extract and honey, and the mash gently put the lid on, and cook on High for 1 hour.
2. Transfer to a blender, pulse well, divide into bowls and serve cold.

per serving: 263 calories,1.4g protein, 27.1g carbohydrates, 14.3g fat, 7.3g fiber, 0mg cholesterol, 11mg sodium, 446mg potassium.

Ginger Pineapple

Preparation time: 10 minutes
Cooking time: 2 hours
Servings: 2

Ingredients:

- 2 cups pineapple, peeled and roughly cubed
- 2 tablespoons honey
- ½ teaspoon ginger, grated

Directions:

1. In your slow cooker, mix the pineapple with ginger, toss, put the lid on and cook on High for 2 hours.
2. Divide into bowls and, sprinkle with honey, serve cold.

per serving: 285 calories,2.4g protein, 42.6g carbohydrates, 14.5g fat, 3.7g fiber, 0mg cholesterol, 12mg sodium, 355mg potassium.

Made in the USA
Coppell, TX
23 September 2023

21905803R00077